When All Hail
Breaks Loose

When All Hail Breaks Loose

Weathering the Storms of Life

Pat Day

Abingdon Press
NASHVILLE

WHEN ALL HAIL BREAKS LOOSE
WEATHERING THE STORMS OF LIFE

Copyright © 2011 by Abingdon Press

Library of Congress Cataloging-in-Publication Data

Day, R. Pat.
When all hail breaks loose : weathering the storms of life / R. Pat Day.
p. cm.
ISBN 978-1-4267-1890-8 (trade pbk. : alk. paper)
1. Suffering—Religious aspects—Christianity. 2. Trust in God—Christianity.
3. Christian life—Methodist authors. I. Title.
BV4909.D39 2011
248.8'6—dc22

2011011627

All scripture quotations unless noted otherwise are from the New Revised Standard Version of the Bible, copyright 1989, Division of Christian Education of the National Council of the Churches of Christ in the United States of America. Used by permission. All rights reserved.

Scripture quotations marked (NIV) are taken from the Holy Bible, NEW INTERNATIONAL VERSION®. Copyright © 1973, 1978, 1984 by International Bible Society. All rights reserved throughout the world. Used by permission of International Bible Society.

Scripture quotations marked (NASB) are taken from the *New American Standard Bible*®, Copyright © 1960, 1962, 1963, 1968, 1971, 1972, 1973, 1975, 1977, 1995 by The Lockman Foundation. Used by permission. (www.Lockman.org)

Scripture quotations marked (NKJV) are taken from the New King James Version®. Copyright © 1982 by Thomas Nelson, Inc. Used by permission. All rights reserved.

Scripture quotations marked (KJV) are from the King James or Authorized Version of the Bible.

Scripture quotations marked (RSV) are taken from the Revised Standard Version of the Bible, copyright 1952 [2nd edition, 1971] by the Division of Christian Education of the National Council of the Churches of Christ in the United States of America. Used by permission. All rights reserved.

11 12 13 14 15 16 17 18 19 20—10 9 8 7 6 5 4 3 2 1
MANUFACTURED IN THE UNITED STATES OF AMERICA

Contents

When All Hail Breaks Loose

ACTS 27:9-29

*"But now I urge you to keep up your courage,
because not one of you will be lost." (Acts 27:22 NIV)*

Storms happen! In fact, life is full of storms—both man-made and natural occurrences. Some are predictable; we can see them coming and have time to prepare for their onslaught. Others blindside us and catch us totally off guard. Many times they simply appear out of nowhere and at the wrong time. Sometimes several major storms hit simultaneously, forcing us to battle them on multiple fronts. They disrupt our plans, our sense of security, and our lives. A storm leaves tremendous devastation in its path. Our lives are never the same after a major storm sweeps through. As we get older, storms seem to come with greater frequency and with even more intensity.

We usually think of a storm as a weather condition that includes a heavy fall of rain, snow, or hail accompanied by high, destructive winds. Tornados, hurricanes, thunderstorms, flash floods, hailstorms, and ice storms immediately come to mind. But storms are much more complex than just the weather-related ones. Storms are crises. They are events and experiences that are powerful, negative, and destructive. We can't control storms. They may be of our own making, or they may involve others. Storms span a wide assortment of events and occurrences, such as betrayal by a close friend, the diagnosis of cancer, a major financial problem, divorce, a serious accident, job loss, an addiction, or the death of a loved one. A storm can even be the death of a dream or a goal that is vitally important to you.

Why do we experience storms in life? Some are self-inflicted—we bring them on ourselves by our poor judgment, bad decisions, and failure to get the help of experts. The captain and crew described in Acts 27 made a terrible mistake in judgment: "When a gentle south wind began to blow, they thought they had obtained what they wanted; so they weighed anchor and sailed along the shore of Crete" (v. 13 NIV). And there are storms that God allows to come into our lives to shake us out of our complacency, to get our attention or in some way bring us closer to him. Many times our storms come into our lives because of the poor choices, mistakes, or accidents of others. But a great many storms just happen. They come out of nowhere, without any warning, and broadside us before we know it. We may have seen a powerful storm coming, but we choose to ignore it. Regardless of where the storms come from, we had better prepare before we encounter them or it will be too late. A close friend constantly reminds me, "Pat, prepare for the worst, look for and expect the best, and in every situation trust God for the rest."

There are three possible outcomes of encountering a storm:

1. a change for the better,
2. a change for the worse,
3. a return to our previous way of living before the storm hit.

A storm is not always a bad or negative experience. It may become a major turning point in life that helps us become better people. Each storm brings with it the possibility and opportunity for positive growth and change. It is not a question of whether we will encounter a storm, but when and how we will navigate and survive the test.

Tragically, many people assume that they are always going to have clear skies, calm seas, and favorable breezes throughout life. They never take the trouble to spend even a short period of time with the Great Captain and with his help prepare for the inevitable and unavoidable storms that are going to come. It is a dangerous risk to venture into life without asking several questions:

- Will my life survive or sink if I encounter the perfect storm?
- If a storm should hit, will I have the resources available to survive the test?
- Will I know how to use these resources in the midst of the chaos, confusion, and complexity of the storm?

In Acts 27 we discover that life is like a voyage at sea. Often our ship encounters unpredictable storms that threaten to destroy us or at least capsize us. Paul and his fellow shipmates are about to encounter the perfect storm, one that threatens to sink their ship and cost them their lives. From their experience, we can learn how Paul faced his storm and overcame it—remaining calm in the midst of calamity.

In our passage we find Paul's ship going through a category five storm called a "nor'easter." The ship and all those aboard are in terrible danger. Fear and panic spread, seizing and immobilizing the captain and the crew. Then an amazing thing happens; Paul, the prisoner, takes command. He calms the crew and restores hope. Paul assures them that they will not die, so they listen for the sound of the waves breaking against the shoreline. Sure enough, they are getting close to land. They prepare to drop anchor so the crew and ship will not be crushed against the breakers. I find in this passage an amazing message of hope and courage for the dark nights of doubt and difficulty. It is a passage of encouragement for each of us as we encounter storms and turbulent seas. What can we learn from this marvelous passage that will help see us through the eye of the storm?

- First, we can learn to recognize how storms affect our lives.
- Second, we can learn to be aware of the phases of the storm.
- Third, we can build a support team that will help us through the storm.
- Fourth, we can learn to replace panic with prayer.
- Finally, we can ask for and hold on to God's anchors in the midst of the storm.

* * * * *

First, Recognize How Storms Affect Our Lives

Storms can cause us to drift. "The ship was caught by the storm and could not head into the wind; so we gave way to it and were driven along" (v. 15 NIV). Millions of people have no direction, purpose, or plan for their lives. The winds of peer pressure, popularity, and pleasure take them to places they thought they would never go. Compromise, conformity, and pleasing the crowd are strong crosscurrents that are difficult to resist. The course of least resistance is to drift—aimlessly, without purpose or direction—until our lives are smashed against the breakers or we run aground on the sandbar of self-destruction.

In the midst of a storm it is easy to forget our goals, our values, our purpose, our commitment to God, and those who really are important to us. It is easy to lose our focus and lose sight of where God wants us to go and what he has called us to do. A famous swimmer was challenged to swim the English Channel. She prepared for several months to accomplish this very daunting goal. On the day that she began her quest the sun was shining brightly. After she had swum for what seemed like an eternity, with the shore finally in sight, a sudden fog bank developed, obscuring her view of the coastline. Finally she quit only several hundred yards short of her goal. When she was asked why she had stopped, she replied, "When I lost vision of the shoreline I simply gave up." The same can happen to any of us. When we lose our vision, it is easy to drift in life. I've known many people who are simply drifting in an important relationship, in their faith, throughout their lives, with disastrous results.

Storms can cause us to discard. "They began to throw the cargo overboard" (v. 18). In the midst of a major crisis it is very tempting to jettison the things that were once very important to us. We become impatient and impulsive. We stop thinking logically and react emotionally. We discard God-given dreams. Important relationships—even with the Lord—go by the wayside. Our moral compass can get lost in the midst of a storm. Even our most important biblical values, beliefs, and principles that we once lived by are replaced by "live for the moment" and "if it feels good, do it." We throw overboard sound decision-making principles that have served us well in the past. But what we discard may be the very thing we need to make it through the storm.

Storms can cause us to despair. "We finally gave up all hope of being saved" (v. 20 NIV). What a powerful statement! One of the last things they lost was hope. When hope is gone, we're finished. Someone once said, "You can live for weeks without food, days without water, minutes without oxygen, but lose hope and you're finished." When we lose hope, we begin to think, *What's the use? Things will never change. It's impossible! Not even God can turn this situation around.*

In the midst of the storm we may forget that God can infuse hope into a hopeless situation. Maybe today our greatest need is a resurrection of hope. Psalm 42:5 states, "Put your hope in God" (NIV). Hope is like a life preserver in the midst of an angry sea—keeping us afloat and keeping our heads up and our eyes fixed on the source of our hope, Jesus Christ.

Storms can cause us to doubt. I'm sure in the midst of the storm not only did those men on Paul's ship lose hope, but they also began to doubt. The question of whether they would make it haunted each of them. The same is true for us; so many times we ask ourselves, *Will I make it?* Only the person in the storm can answer this question. But one of the ways God helps us is by sending someone into our lives who has survived a similar storm. Just discovering and accepting that there is life on the other side of the storm are tremendously encouraging and hopeful. God can transform our doubts and turn question marks into exclamation points of certainty and faith.

* * * * *

Second, Be Aware of the Phases of the Storm

Impact is the first phase.

We are hit with the full power and intensity of the storm. This phase may last for a few hours to a few days based on the severity and strength of the crisis. It is like being hit with a baseball bat. We are stunned by the impact of the bad news, traumatic event, or unexpected blow. We feel numb and disoriented. It is difficult, if not impossible, to make decisions. We try to shake the cobwebs out of our heads. We think, *This can't be happening. It's all a bad dream. I'll wake up and it will all be over!* But it isn't.

Withdrawal or confusion is phase two.

We battle feelings of grief, anger, guilt, and fear intermittently. It is hard to think or speak. Our thinking is fuzzy, and our minds are dull. Certainly, now is not the time to make major decisions. At this point we need to depend on others we can trust to help us make the day-to-day decisions we face.

Adjustment is phase three.

This phase takes several weeks, months, and in some cases years. We slowly climb out of the valley into which the storm has driven us. We begin to see a tiny ray of hope for the future. I have heard many people complain,

"My life is never going to be the same." That is true, but we have the opportunity to choose how our lives will be in the future. Positive, hope-filled thoughts help us envision a new and brighter future. We are becoming new people.

Resolution is phase four.

We will be different after the storm is over. We will be better or bitter, closer to God or farther away from him. We gradually experience hope and happiness again. We have a choice to make: move on and become a new person, or continue to dwell in the pain of the past. We can choose to continue to live shackled to the pain of the past or choose to close the old chapters in our lives and allow God to write new ones.

* * * * * *

Third, Build a Support Team
That Will Help Us through the Storm

God uses other people to help us survive our storms. Regardless of how strong or how independent we are, sooner or later we will come face-to-face with something or someone we cannot battle alone. For many years my life sailed along fairly smoothly. Sure, I had my ups and downs, and there were always some bumps in the road, but nothing that the Lord and I couldn't handle together. Then in 2005 my world fell apart. A thirty-year marriage ended, my dad died, and two major hurricanes hit our state, just to mention a few of the storms I faced that year. Through it all I discovered how important my family and friends really are. God brought into my life people who helped me make it through the storm. For years I had been the one who was ministering to other people, but now the tables were turned. I needed God, but I also needed others to minister to me.

Our support team will be made up of **family and friends**—new friends as well as friends from our past—who have experienced similar crises. God will bring into our lives experts in dealing with our particular storms: counselors, doctors, attorneys, and mentors. We must not be too proud to avail ourselves of God's angels disguised in human form! Some of them will be with us for a season, others will be there for a specific reason, and some will be there for a lifetime.

The Lord never meant for us to go through the storms of life by ourselves. It's amazing the strength, support, and courage that come to us when we know someone else loves us and is praying for us. We do not go through our storms alone—unless we choose to do so.

Our support team should be made up of people who are **trustworthy**. They know how to keep a confidence.

When we share with them, we have no fear that the information will appear on the front page of the newspaper. Our support team is composed of people who love and pray for us and who want what's best for us. Our team members are **genuinely interested** in us and will listen without interrupting with well-intended advice. They care enough to speak the truth in love. Good team members help us analyze the problem, determine the facts, and see the crisis or problem for what it really is. They are there **to encourage, to help, and to believe in us** even when we don't believe in ourselves. They help us look beyond the storm to see the possibilities for the future. I don't see how anyone can survive a major storm without this type of support team. We must allow others the blessing of helping us.

* * * * *

Fourth, Replace Panic with Prayer

Prayer is such an important part of making it through the perfect storm that I have dedicated an entire chapter to the significance of prayer. Acts 27:23-24 states, "Last night an angel of the God whose I am and whom I serve stood beside me and said, 'Do not be afraid'" (NIV). Fear immobilizes us. It causes panic and exaggerates the severity of the situation. Panic makes us feel isolated, helpless, powerless, and overwhelmed by the intensity of the storm.

In my years as a minister dealing with the crises that people go through, I have learned to depend heavily on prayer. I have prayed many, many times for people to have peace, poise, and God's abiding presence in their lives.

I have learned that prayer opens the door to God's creative possibilities.

I pray specifically for his guidance and his wisdom. We need to set aside time each day for periods of prayer. After we talk to the Lord about our problems or crises, we must meditate and sit quietly and wait for him to give us thoughts, insights, ideas, and steps that we need to take to get through the storms.

Prayer enables us to see things differently.

Prayer enables us to see things from God's perspective. Philippians 4:6 is a guideline for positive praying: "In everything, by prayer and petition, with thanksgiving, present your requests to God" (NIV). "With thanksgiving" is a way of affirming the goodness and greatness of God. Praise and thanksgiving in the midst of a storm open us to the flow of the Lord's spirit and power.

I've often been asked, "How can I thank God for a storm or crisis?" Storms are so difficult, powerful, and destructive. Storms crush. In the process of crushing, they often refine and purify our lives. Each time we are tempted to think negatively or complain, we can use prayer to replace those thoughts with positive, faith-filled thoughts giving thanks to God—not necessarily for the storm, but for the strength, courage, and grace that he will give us to enable us to endure and pass through the storm. First Thessalonians 5:18 states, "Give thanks in all circumstances, for this is God's will for you in Christ Jesus" (NIV).

* * * * *

Finally, Ask for and Hold on to God's Anchors in the Midst of the Storm

At the height of the storm Paul calms the crew and restores hope. He assures them that they will not die, so they begin to listen for the sound of the waves breaking along the shoreline. They realize that they are getting close to land. Now follows one of my favorite passages in the Bible, Acts 27:29: "Fearing that we would be dashed against the rocks, they dropped four anchors from the stern and prayed for daylight" (NIV). I find here an amazing message of hope and courage for the dark nights of doubt, difficulties, and despair that all of us encounter sooner or later. The Lord's message to Paul provides us with four vital anchors to hold our ship off the reef as we pray for the darkness of an impossible situation to be lifted and for morning to break. What are these four anchors?

The first anchor is the Lord's presence.
"An angel of . . . God . . . stood beside me." As we read and study the book of Acts, we see this anchor in Paul's life. The Lord's presence has kept Paul's life off the rocks many times before. In 2 Corinthians 11:16-33 Paul gives a detailed account of all of his trials, tests, and tribulations. Each time, the Lord's presence has sustained him and gotten him through the ordeal. I have discovered that to know God's presence is with me, even though it might seem that everything is all wrong, gives me courage and confidence that he is still in control.

The second anchor is God's purpose.
The Lord gave Paul the assurance of a divine destiny: "Paul, you must stand trial before Caesar" (Acts 27:24 NIV). Knowing God has a plan and a purpose for our lives is one of the greatest anchors that we can have. He wants to reassure us that we are not accidents or afterthoughts. God has a plan and a purpose for your life: " 'For I know the plans I have for you,' declares

the LORD, 'plans to prosper you and not to harm you, plans to give you hope and a future'" (Jeremiah 29:11 NIV). God would protect Paul for the fulfillment of his divine purpose. The Lord offers to each one of us the anchor of a divine destiny. Absolutely nothing or no one can stop the person who truly feels "called by God" to do what he or she is doing. Once we are sure why we are alive, we can encounter any storm triumphantly.

The third anchor is God's promise.

Can we trust his promise? Trying times are times to try trusting God with our lives. It was this anchor that allowed Paul to say, "I can do all things through him who strengthens me" (Philippians 4:13). This is especially true when we experience a storm of fear. The angel said to Paul, "Do not be afraid" (Acts 27:24). Paul, like each of us, had a choice to trust and believe God's promise, or to question, doubt, and disbelieve his word.

The fourth anchor is the power of God.

God's power is greater than any storm we will ever face. Paul describes this promise in Philippians 3:10: "I want to know Christ and the power of his resurrection." Resurrection power—the power to bring life from death. Isn't that the type of power that we need in our lives today? God's power makes all these other anchors secure.

The dark night of the storm is so long that we begin to wonder whether dawn will ever break. But many have believed in Jesus Christ's power. Without his power living in us we will be constantly tossed to and fro in the sea of life.

We all have the same four anchors. Morning finally did come. The ship's passengers and crew were not drowned. All of them made it to the shore safely. The Lord was faithful to his promise, and Paul could go to Rome to be his faithful witness there. And so can we today remain faithful, steadfast in our faith in the risen Christ. I love the words of the old song:

> In times like these you need an anchor.
> Be very sure, be very sure your anchor holds and grips
>   the solid rock.
> —Ruth Caye Jones, 1944

God says, "I am with you. You can make it!" Through our faith and prayer, his strength will stabilize us. With a loving support team's help, we will find courage and confidence to move through our crises. Those storms cannot ultimately defeat God's plan for us.

* * * * *

Are Our Lives Unsinkable?

Are our lives unsinkable? When the storms come, will we sink or survive? I remember, as a ten- or twelve-year-old boy, getting the kids together in the neighborhood to make a boat. My family had gotten a new air conditioner, and the empty wooden crate would make, in my opinion, an excellent seaworthy vessel with just the right adaptations. So we took tar and sealed all the cracks that we could see. We worked and worked until I thought our boat was seaworthy.

Then came the day for the launch. We had to drag our boat to the nearest pond behind my house. My dad's cows had to come along, too, curious what these crazy kids were up to. Then came the moment of truth— would it sink or float? That question was quickly answered. As we pushed our little air conditioner crate boat into the pond and I got in to row it, within seconds water started coming in from every direction. A few short seconds later, the USS *Day* sank to the bottom of the pond. Even the cows were laughing as they walked off after our less than spectacular launch! I've thought a lot about that boyhood adventure for years. How like my boat are so many people's lives. On the outside they appear safe, secure, and seaworthy. Just let a little storm come along, though, and they begin to sink. Just let the wind blow and the waves strike, and their lives quickly sink. Is my life unsinkable? Will my life pass the test when all hail breaks loose? Is my faith strong enough to keep me on top and keep me from sinking?

Living with fortitude and perseverance, we can know that God's purpose will be complete, and his plan for our lives will be fulfilled. There is a reason for it all, and we are going to make it safely!

CHAPTER ONE

Faith It until You Make It

2 CORINTHIANS 5:7

For we walk by faith, not by sight.

At the climax of the movie *Indiana Jones and the Last Crusade*, Indiana has to pass three supreme tests to reach the Holy Grail and save his dying father. The first test is "the breath of God." As he walks down a corridor, Indiana must bow down at precisely the right moment to keep from having his head cut off by large revolving metal blades. The second test is "the word of God." Indiana must walk on just the right stones—the ones that spell God's name in Latin—to keep from falling through the floor to his death. But the third test, "the path of God," is the most difficult. Indiana comes to the edge of a large chasm—about a hundred feet across and a thousand feet down.

21

If I were Indiana, I would call "time out" on this test.

On the other side of the chasm is the doorway to the Holy Grail. The instructions say, "Only in the leap from the lion's head will he prove his worth." Jones says to himself, "It's impossible. Nobody can jump this." Then he realizes that this test requires a leap of faith. His father says, "You must believe, boy. You must believe!" Even though every nerve and fiber of his being screams that he must not do it, Indiana walks to the edge of the cliff . . . lifts his foot . . . and then steps out into thin air, hoping that somehow he won't crash to the floor of the deep chasm. Instead of falling, he is upheld by an invisible force. This is a powerful picture of what faith is all about. Without faith it is impossible to please God, but when we take that first step of faith and then another and another, our confidence and trust will grow with each step.

The beginning of a new year, a new day, a new job, a new relationship, or a new project is an excellent time for a faith checkup. Our success will largely be defined by our ability to **faith it until we make it.** A life characterized by faith or a life paralyzed by fear— which will we choose? Will we choose as Indiana Jones did and venture out, or will we simply call for "time out"?

Faith Is as Essential to Achievement as Air Is to Breathing

Faith is the key that unlocks the door to God's blessings and favor. He challenges us to trust him before we actually see the results. We are reminded in the Scriptures that without faith it is impossible to please God. The Christian life is an ongoing learning experience based on our ability and willingness to trust God as our divine provider and promise keeper.

In 2 Corinthians 5:7 we read that we are to live by faith and not by sight. Without a doubt, God is able to do immeasurably more than all we ask or imagine (Ephesians 3:20). God wants to create great things through us and our faith. While only **God can** see the number of apples in a single seed, with the eyes of faith **we can** see immense possibilities. Faith gives us the peace to imagine, to believe that we can do it, and to know that God will provide the resources necessary to make the dream become reality.

When I read about the great men and women of faith in the Bible, I'm inspired and challenged by their ability to trust God for the seemingly impossible. For example, "By faith Abraham, when called to go to a place he would later receive as his inheritance, obeyed and went, even though he did not know where he was going"

(Hebrews 11:8 NIV). My faith grows and is strengthened when I read these words. God said to Abraham, "Go, leave the security of the known and take my unseen hand into the unknown." How simple, yet how profound!

If we choose to walk by faith and not by sight, it will not be easy. The faint of heart cannot walk by faith, but the faint of heart are not often successful either. If we dare to do great things for God's glory, we will be tried and tested—count on it! But as our faith grows stronger, the greater will be our determination to prevail. David Foster writes, "Faith is the ability to trust in advance that which will only make sense in reverse." How much faith do I need? How much faith is required? How do I build my faith?

Faith It until You Make It

In my life I have found I can **faith it until I make it** by working to follow these biblical principles:

- First, I *choose* to move from a risk-free safe zone into the riskier faith zone.
- Second, I *surrender* my fears to God.
- Third, I *learn* that problems and obstacles are a part of God's plan for building my faith.
- Fourth, I *trust* God's promise.
- Finally, I *persist* until I break through to a new level of faith.

* * * * *

Moving from a Risk-free Safe Zone into the Riskier Faith Zone

All of us have what could be called "a spiritual comfort zone." A comfort zone is safe, easy, predictable, and manageable. In our comfort zones we are able to live and perform basically under our own power. We can handle whatever comes our way by our own intellect and our own planning. Life is very predictable, maybe even monotonous. There are no real surprises. We risk nothing. We choose to play it safe. We are comfortable, safe, and secure without any threats to our rather mundane existence. When we think of the past, we remember our failed attempts to risk anything very big because we fell flat on our faces. For the most part, we leave God out of our lives or compartmentalize or quarantine them so as not to intrude or affect the areas of our lives that we think are important.

Only one way is available for us to escape the unproductive comfort zone: we must choose to live daily in the faith zone. This takes a risk—a leap of faith. Each of us must admit: "I cannot do this in my own strength any longer. I really need to begin to trust God." God wants each of us to live in the faith zone. He will orchestrate situations, circumstances, and events that will stretch us again and again. He wants us to move from the safety of the shallow water into the unknown of the deep water of faith. There, in the depth of faith, is where God lives.

That unknown might come as a crisis, a crossroads, or a challenge that makes us so miserable, so desperate, and so restless that business as usual is no longer acceptable. The disciples fished all night without any success. Then Jesus told them to put their nets out into the deep water. John 21:6 tells us that they caught such an enormous amount of fish, the boat almost sank. *Had they not attempted to risk everything, they would have continued to catch absolutely nothing.* Like the disciples, it is time for us to move out of the safe zone into the faith zone.

It is okay to say no, but be forewarned: we will miss God's best for our lives. We will never get to see what God really could have done in our lives. Remember, the faith zone is where miracles happen. When we deliberately make the decision to enter the faith zone, we will feel very uneasy, unsafe, out of control, and uncomfortable at times. But we will come to depend on the Lord in a way that we never could have done in the safe zone. "Without faith it is impossible to please God," Paul tells us in Hebrews 11:6. His will for us is to be constantly and consistently dependent on him for everything. Faith is not our responsibility; it is our response to

God's ability. And like Indiana Jones, we can learn to respond to his ability and **surrender our fears to God.**

* * * * *

Surrendering My Fears to God

Fear has three basic traits that we need to acknowledge. Then we need to find ways to think beyond these characteristics that limit our opportunities for success in our lives:

Fear is contagious. We catch it from others. In late 2008, a worldwide economic crisis resulted in tremendous losses in both the stock market and in personal wealth. An epidemic of fear magnified the effects of this crisis.

Fear is limiting. It will keep us from doing what God wants because of our sense of inadequacy and powerlessness. Fear has tremendous limiting power over each of us. When we are afraid, we will never attempt what God is asking us to be or to do.

Fear is draining. Fear has a way of stealing our strength, destroying our dreams, and robbing us of our power and possibilities for the future. Fear sucks the very life out of us. It destroys the very best within us.

Fear disrupts faith because it is the biggest obstacle to trusting and obeying God. In 1933 President Franklin D. Roosevelt said to the American public in the dark hours of the Great Depression, "The only thing we have to fear is fear itself." In other words, we keep life carefully confined within the boundaries of what we are confident of being able to handle by ourselves. Our fear of failure or of taking a big risk keeps us from anything that we cannot control or that we cannot safely foresee. We place self-imposed limitations on what we can do as well as on what we think God can do. We have calculated, reasoned, and predicted the outcome based upon our human resources, experiences, and limitations. In reality, we don't need God to do the possible. We need, instead, to let go of all those artificial protective barriers we have established. We need to let God have our fears and move into the faith zone.

Faith doesn't mean the absence of fear. It means having the courage to go ahead, right alongside the fear, remembering **that problems and obstacles are a part of God's plan for building our faith.**

We feed our faith by asking the Holy Spirit to direct us to the promises in the Bible that apply to our problems. Then we can begin to obey the conditions that are attached to those promises.

- We believe and expect God's provision and faith.
- We praise and thank God in advance for his miraculous provision or intervention.
- We verbalize our faith by speaking his promise as prediction.
- We maintain a constant attitude of trust in the Lord and not in ourselves.
- We associate and worship with positive, faith-filled people as a way of building our faith.

Now let's ask ourselves what daring, amazing thing we'd attempt when we know we cannot possibly fail.

* * * * *

Learning That Problems and Obstacles Are a Part of God's Plan for Building My Faith

God is the master designer, and he has a master plan that is uniquely suited for our lives. Obstacles and problems are vital parts of his teaching us faith development. Initially when we come face-to-face with a major problem, crisis, or obstacle, we may feel discouraged, defeated, and depressed. We may be tempted to question, doubt, or even become angry with God because of his leading us into this challenging situation. But every stage of our faith development depends on God. What obstacles are you facing that are challenging your faith and causing you to become fearful and give up? Many obstacles can hit us: loss of a job, financial reversals, health problems, or a bad relationship. We may be terribly discouraged by these problems and wonder, "What's the use?"

The very problem that has the possibility to destroy, discourage, and defeat us contains the resources that will nourish our faith. Problems and obstacles become stepping-stones to a stronger faith. They become stair steps for moving up in life. Problems provide the platform on which God can work his miracles. My faith has grown in the face of the challenges that I've encountered. I've learned that great faith is neither possible nor required in the absence of great problems. If we know how faith works, challenges are the best things that can happen to us. Andraé Crouch wrote a wonderful little chorus many years ago that has helped me. He sings, "Through it all, through it all, I've learned to trust in Jesus."

By faith, I've known that the bigger the problem, the greater the possibilities and the greater the blessing. Adversity has within it the seeds of advantage. Problems give birth to possibilities, and everything turns on the hinge of faith. When a God-given opportunity comes along disguised as a problem, it is God's gift to us. What we do with it is our gift to God.

Zig Ziglar writes after the death of his daughter,

> There is no grief that I have experienced that has come close to my grief over the loss of our child. Throughout our months and years of grieving, faith has been the redeeming force that has enabled us to bear the pain and continue to live in victory. . . . The very process of grief is given to us by a loving heavenly Father. God uses grief to heal us, strengthen us in our faith, and cause us to grow in our relationship with Him. (*Confessions of a Grieving Christian* [Nashville: Thomas Nelson, 1999], p. 2)

It is in the furnace of adversity that our character is refined and our faith is strengthened. Sir Edmund Hillary became the first man to reach the summit of Mount Everest. He had failed several times. After one failure, he shook his fist at the mountain and said, "You have defeated me, but I will return, and I will defeat you, because you can't get any bigger, but I can!" And he did accomplish the goal of climbing Mount Everest in 1953.

The best way to learn about the power of faith is to actually place ourselves in a situation that forces us to trust God for big things. Jesus promised in Matthew 17:20, "I tell you the truth, if you have faith as small as a mustard seed, you can say to this mountain, 'Move from here to there' and it will move. Nothing will be impossible for you" (NIV). God doesn't require great faith; he asks only that we **trust his promises.**

* * * * *

Trusting God's Promise

My dad was a peanut broker. Each spring, like farmers all over the world, his customers took the risk of buying seed and fertilizer, plowing their fields, and planting their crops. Those peanut crops resulting from the farmers' risks provided support and financial security for our family so that I, as a young boy, could make choices about the direction for my life. A farmer cannot possibly begin to expect a harvest until the seeds are planted in the spring. The same is true with our faith. We must act before God will ever bless. We must plant the seeds of faith in rich soil and nurture them and water them on a daily basis so that our faith will continue to grow and produce a harvest of a hundredfold.

We live in a world where trust is at an all-time low. Promise keeping and truth telling have fallen on tough times, especially in the business, investment, and political worlds—even in the religious world. Many millions of people have been betrayed by trusting unscrupulous people to invest their money properly. But this is not the case with our faith in God. What he says, he will do. **The greater the problem, the greater the promise.**

When God gives us a promise, we must listen to his voice and obey him completely. "Faith is believing what we do not see. The reward of faith is to see what we be-lieve," according to Saint Augustine, a saint of the early church. Listening requires reading the Bible—his word to us. But it also involves being still before him, listen-ing to his still, quiet voice, and then recording what he says we should do.

I normally keep a notebook close by so that I can jot down what I believe God is telling me. Faith requires obedience if we are to solve our problems. I pray for wisdom and discernment. I ask God for his action plan, and when he reveals it, I write down what I hear. Once we have his plan, we must act by faith to build upon that plan. James 1:6-7 states, "But let him ask in faith, with no doubting, for he who doubts is like a wave of the sea driven and tossed by the wind. For let not that man sup-pose that he will receive anything from the Lord" (NKJV). In Mark 11:24 we read, "Whatever things you ask when you pray, believe that you receive them, and you will have them" (NKJV).

In the summer of 2005, my dad went home to be with the Lord. He was my hero and my best friend. He was a very successful businessman who chose to live mod-estly. He did not have the toys or symbols of success that so many people flaunt. But the one thing he took great pride in was a diamond ring that he liked to wear. When he died, the ring was given to me. For months I refused to wear it. Then one day I felt it was time to start wearing the ring in his honor, even though I did not feel worthy to do so. When I tried it on, it seemed to be a little loose—maybe a size or so too large. But I chose to wear it anyway.

The next morning I dressed for church, but I could not find the ring! Of course, as soon as church was over, I turned my apartment upside down. Still no ring! I searched high and low but still could not find it. I began to pray. How could I, in such a short twenty-four hours, have lost Dad's ring? I called my aunt and told her what had happened and asked her to pray that I would find it. I then called my son to come and help me look for it. I began to pray frantically.

I searched with fear welling up inside me, but still no ring. Just as I started to look again in the apartment, a thought flashed in my mind. It was strong, so real, so powerful: *Look in the Dumpster!* I thought, *You've got to be kidding! I'm not going to look in the Dumpster; it's filthy and stinks terribly. What would people think if they saw me rummaging through the Dumpster on a Sunday afternoon?* So I quickly dismissed the thought.

But it came back again, this time more powerful, more intense: *Look in the Dumpster. If you don't, you'll never see your dad's ring again!* Talk about an inward struggle! I put on my jeans and rubber boots and started emptying the Dumpster. By Sunday afternoon an apartment Dumpster is filled with the trash from the weekend activities. This one was filled to the top. I unloaded bags and bags of stinky, dirty trash. I got so desperate that I crawled into the Dumpster. Then I heard a voice outside asking, "Dr. Day, is that you in the Dumpster?" I looked up and saw a young man who had been in church that morning. Talk about embarrassed! I can only imagine what he thought, probably something like this: *Things must be getting really tough if our pastor has to rummage through the Dumpster!*

Finally I had emptied enough of the Dumpster to stand up in it—but still no ring. I was getting close to the last bag when I recognized a trash bag from my apartment. It dawned on me that I had put it in the Dumpster the previous afternoon. My son began to look through it as I searched through the yucky water in the bottom of the Dumpster. I will never forget his cry of astonishment when he yelled, "Dad, you won't believe it, but I found Dedaddy's ring!" I broke into tears. I was reminded of Jesus' passage in Luke 15 when the lost coin was found. I thanked God for his help in finding Dad's ring. On the following Monday, my good friend sized the ring, and I now wear it daily as a symbol of my earthly father's love for me and my heavenly Father's answer to prayer. **The better we know God, the more we will trust him.**

The way to know his trustworthiness is to risk obeying him consistently day in and day out. That is, we must persist until we break through to a new level of faith. We must remember: we can if we think we can. There is nothing magical or mystical about the power of belief. The belief that Paul claimed in Philippians 4:13, "I can do all things through him who strengthens me," is an expression of faith that guarantees the power, the skill, and the energy to meet whatever challenge we have set for ourselves. When we believe with Christ, "I can do it," the *how* develops. Henry Ford once said, "I am looking for a lot of men who have an infinite capacity not to know what can't be done." A strong belief triggers the mind to forge ways and means of how to do it. Belief that we can succeed makes others place confidence in us.

Sooner or later every one of us will experience a life-jolting, faith-shattering situation. Everything in our lives will be shaken to the very core. Even our belief about God and his nature may be shaken. Everything that was once secure and safe will start falling apart. We may feel a little like the woman who came into my office one morning and said, "The only thing that's holding me together today is my hair spray."

"Shake, rattle, and roll," Jerry Lee Lewis sang. That's what life will do to us from time to time. But we are not destined to crash and burn. At these times, living life is somewhat like praying as I drive through a terrible storm. I move forward faithfully and slowly, and finally, when I emerge from the storm, I feel amazing calmness and peace. **I persist until I break through to a new level of faith.**

* * * * *

Persisting to a New Level of Faith

A man had had a lifelong dream of being a writer, but his life was on a downward spiral, leaving him in a pit of alcoholism that resulted in the loss of his house, his wife, his daughter, and his job. He was on his way to buy a gun and end his life when he found the book that changed his life: *Success through a Positive Mental Attitude* by W. Clement Stone and Napoleon Hill. He applied to Stone's insurance company for a job. As his life began to turn around, he became the editor of *Success Unlimited* and wrote a classic work, *The Greatest Salesman in the World*, which was published and has been read by literally tens of millions of people. His name was Og Mandino. What a loss to so many of us if he had not persevered!

The Greatest Measure of Character

"I can't do it. It's impossible. It's foolish even to try. I might as well give up and quit." Often I have made such statements at different turning points in my life. Everyone suffers defeats; you cannot always win. The greatest measure of true character is how we handle ourselves when defeat comes.

Consider two outstanding racehorses, Man o' War and John P. Grier. Man o' War had never been defeated in a race. As the race began, John P. Grier took the lead, which he held throughout most of the race. In the closing few lengths the jockey on Man o' War did something that he had never done before: he struck Man o' War with his whip, and this action startled the horse. Man o' War reached down deep inside himself and found new strength and new power that ultimately led him to victory. John P. Grier's career was basically over. Someone once asked, "What happened to this great horse?" One of the experts replied, "He let defeat defeat him."

When we get knocked down in life, we must get back up. I learned early in sports that the most dangerous play on the football field is when you are knocked down and are lying on the ground. You are safest when you are on your feet, competing. A champion boxer was once asked about his secret for success. He replied, "When I got knocked down, I got back up and fought just one more round!"

Ten-year-old Glenn Cunningham and a friend made a terrible mistake. They poured gasoline in the family's cookstove, which caused a tremendous explosion and killed the friend. Glenn was more fortunate, even though the accident almost cost him one leg. Each time the doctors said that the leg needed to be amputated, Glenn asked them to give it one more day. After a great deal of surgery and a lengthy period of rehabilitation, his leg was saved. As he recovered, one leg was a full two and one-half inches shorter than the other, and his right foot was badly damaged. Yet through his persistence, Glenn Cunningham became one of the greatest track stars in history.

Many of us are not utilizing the faith we have. God will not give us greater faith until we realize the faith we now have. We must exercise our faith by trusting him for something so big that we cannot possibly succeed unless he intervenes. John Wesley told young preachers, "If you don't have faith, then preach it until you get it!" Many of us have heard the phrase, "Fake it until you make it." In other words, we should act as if something is already a reality. If I can see myself as the person I hope to become, sooner or later I will not be an actor. I actually will become that person. We must act with confidence, assurance, and conviction. The subconscious mind can't distinguish between what is real and what is fantasy. Faith is visualizing and seeing what is not yet real.

When we are going through a life-shaking, life-shattering situation, we can trust God for a break-through—his breakthrough in his way, in his timing, and through his provision. Our faith in the Lord enables us to break through our difficulties into the next level of faith. Persistence, perseverance, and determination to prevail are required. The Bible speaks of many levels of faith: a measure of faith, little faith, great faith, or mountain-moving faith. God is working in each of our lives to help us learn to live by faith and not by sight.

Our actions reflect our belief. What we do determines what we believe. By taking even the smallest steps, we are communicating to ourselves and to the world that we believe in ourselves and our dream. In the beginning we may not feel very brave or confident, much less unstoppable. By taking confident concrete actions, we will be assured and poised eventually. Every action we take raises our self-esteem and our self-confidence. We are no longer sitting, waiting, and hoping for something magical to happen. We are the co-creators of the miracle. In Mark 9:23 we are told, "Everything is possible for him who believes" (NIV). We have that choice: Do we choose to **faith it until we make it**?

Worth Remembering

- "Everything is possible for him who believes" (Mark 9:23 NIV).
- Faith is not my responsibility; it is my response to God's ability.
- "Faith is believing what we do not see. The reverse of faith is to see what we believe" (Saint Augustine).
- "Whatever things you ask when you pray, believe that you receive them, and you will have them" (Mark 11:24 NKJV).

Questions

1. When was a time that you took a risk and trusted God?
2. Where is God asking you or your church to move out of your comfort zone and really trust him?
3. What holds you back? What obstacles and fears do you need to overcome?
4. How has God helped you overcome a major problem in the past?
5. Share a time when God answered your prayer.

Power Connection

Lord, help me trust in your divine provision and power. Give me the faith to see your invisible hand working in my life. Forgive me when my fears and doubts cause me to question and I fail to trust you. Amen.

CHAPTER TWO

Pray through It

LUKE 11:9-10

"So I say to you, Ask, and it will be given you; search,
and you will find; knock, and the door will be opened for you.
For everyone who asks receives, and everyone who searches finds,
and for everyone who knocks, the door will be opened."

Several years ago I was going through the darkest time in my entire life. Around the clock I battled fear, insecurity, and a sense of helplessness and hopelessness. In the midst of my disruptive storm a close friend gave me a wooden cross that fit perfectly in my hand. When I felt frightened or those feelings of dread overwhelmed me, I held that cross and prayed until those feelings were dispelled. Many nights I went to sleep holding the cross, and in the morning I woke up and saw it still there in my hand. The cross gave me great assurance and great confidence that regardless of how bad the storm might be, God was going to see me through. When we face storms in our lives, we may ask, Does prayer really work?

What Prayer Does God Answer?

In 1970 *Time* magazine selected as its cover the picture of the three Apollo 13 astronauts—heads bowed, hands folded, shoulders drooping, thanking God for their safe homecoming. I vividly remember the space flight of Apollo 13. Others among us have relived that week with the endangered astronauts through the movie *Apollo 13*, directed by Ron Howard. An explosion on board forced a change in Apollo 13's plan to land on the moon and shifted the mission into a frenzied endeavor to return the astronauts safely home. On the ground, mission control teams worked frantically to come up with an alternative that could replace damaged equipment. People around the world began praying for the safety and survival of those young men. When they finally splashed down in the Pacific Ocean, the world watched the NASA chaplain offer a prayer of thanks for their safe return. In response to a question from someone in the press, astronaut Jack Swigert replied, "If you are asking if we prayed, I can certainly say we did! We think that the prayers of those around the world helped us get back safely." Needless to say, nothing motivates us to get serious about our prayer life quicker than a major crisis. We may ask, What type of prayer does God answer?

Real prayer is not an attempt to rub a divine Aladdin's lamp and make God become a celestial genie or a divine valet hopefully fulfilling all of our wishes and whims. Rather, real prayer brings our will into alignment with God's will. Real prayer helps us see the problem from God's perspective. **One thing is certain: God always answers real prayer.** Most of us have had the experience of praying for a specific problem, and the answer didn't seem to come, leaving us disillusioned and questioning the validity of prayer. Some of us have been fortunate to know someone who caused us to really and truly feel the presence of God when he or she prayed. We knew that the person had an intimate relationship with God—a hotline to heaven.

When I moved to Marshall, Texas, I met a wonderful Christian man I'll call Nate. Brother Nate had an unbelievable prayer life. When he prayed, I knew I was in the presence of God. His prayer life had been developed over years and years of meeting God daily in prayer. His example challenged me to begin to take seriously my prayer life. Over the years my prayer life has deepened and strengthened. I am not where I want to be, but thank God, I'm not where I used to be. I've discovered that people like Brother Nate have chosen to tap into the most powerful force on earth—prayer power. Prayer power is not so much based on the language we

use, the volume, or even the length of the prayer. Prayer
power engages the heart of God and touches both the
person praying and the person being prayed for.

God's Personal Invitation

In his book *Prayer, the Mightiest Force in the World*,
Frank Laubach claims that so many times we neglect
tapping into this unbelievable resource. He talks about
people who risk praying through their problems, knowing that they are praying to a God of power. It is hard
to believe that the God of the universe extends a sacred
invitation to bring our thoughts, our dreams, as well as
our problems into his presence. Jesus summarized his
invitation in John 16:23-24: "In that day you will no
longer ask me anything. I tell you the truth, my Father
will give you whatever you ask in my name. Until now
you have not asked for anything in my name. Ask and
you will receive, and your joy will be complete" (NIV).

Just imagine: if we really believed that promise, it
would be like God giving us a spiritual credit card so
that we can make withdrawals from his storehouse.
When our requests align and match his purpose and his
will, we are gratefully allowed to make a withdrawal.
Jesus gives us a personal invitation to pray our way
through every difficulty. Too often we are afraid to ask
God for anything. We are afraid that we might not be

answered or that we might be praying for the wrong thing. So we play it safe. We never go out on a limb; we never risk anything. Why don't we try asking God for something so big that unless he intervenes, we are destined to fail? As I have worked to develop my prayer life and experience his interventions, I have tried to practice the following principles:

- First, I passionately seek to know God intimately.
- Second, I humbly ask for God's help.
- Third, I believe God is bigger than any problem that I encounter.
- Fourth, I keep my mental and spiritual contact points clean so that God's power can operate in my life.
- Finally, I pray my way through every difficulty until there is a release or an answer.

Let's explore together how purposeful practice of these behaviors can increase our prayer power.

* * * * *

Seeking to Know God Intimately

Intimacy with the infinite is the basis for real prayer power. Jeremiah 29:13 records the words of God: "You will seek me and find me when you seek me with all your heart" (NIV). This passage describes a sense of desperation, a sense of hunger and thirst in finding God in a real and personal way. We read in Psalm 42:1-2,

> As the deer pants for streams of water,
>   so my soul pants for you, O God.
> My soul thirsts for God, for the living God.
>   When can I go and meet with God? (NIV)

Powerful prayers are not hollow, empty words but are intimate and heartfelt. When we have a burning desire to know God intimately and spend time developing the love relationship with him, we transform our prayer life. Intimacy is developed by setting aside intentional time to be with God, that is, a quiet time or a daily devotional time of both quality and quantity.

More than forty years ago I began a daily quiet time, and it has resulted in getting to know God in a way that I never could have imagined. There is no such thing as instant intimacy with God. Just as our relationships with our spouses or close friends require intentionality, our relationship with God requires intentionality and making that relationship a priority for our time so that nothing else gets in its way. In fact, to help us build the habit of regular time with God, we might put it on our daily calendars: an appointment with God—do not interrupt.

Paul had a burning passion to know God intimately. In Philippians 3:10 he states, "I want to know Christ and the power of his resurrection and the fellowship of sharing in his sufferings" (NIV). More than anything else, Paul wanted a deep, personal relationship with Jesus Christ. In the model prayer, the Lord's Prayer, Jesus began by saying, "Our Father." The word for "father" in the Greek is *abba*, which means the most intimate term of endearment, such as "daddy" would be in our language today. If a relationship with someone is distant or nonexistent, asking for help from that person when we encounter a major problem can be extremely difficult. It makes me think of driving through a strange city at three o'clock in the morning and my car breaks down. I remember a college classmate lives in that town, but I haven't had any contact with that person in more than thirty years. Am I likely to be willing to call and ask him for help?

When we are close to God, it is much easier to ask for his help than if we have no relationship with him at all. In fact, God invites us to come to him with the same dependency of a child who asks her daddy to tie her shoe or tend to her scraped knee. God wants us to turn from the problem and focus entirely on him. Our heavenly Father loves us deeply and wants nothing but his best for us. There is absolutely nothing that we can do to make him stop loving us. Although we may not have talked to God in many years, now is the time to begin a new relationship with him. He will welcome us with open arms as we **humbly ask for his help**.

* * * * *

Asking for God's Help

Spiritual power flows from personal brokenness. God's presence equals God's power. Abraham Lincoln once said, "I've been driven many times to my knees by the overwhelming conviction that I have nowhere else to go." When we come to God in humility, bankrupt, desperate, realizing we have no place else to turn, God pays special attention. When we are broken, we will pour out our hearts to God rather than try to persuade him to do what we want. Prayers that are birthed in brokenness and desperation come from people at the end of their ropes. King David understood this quite well when he wrote in Psalm 51:17, "A broken and contrite heart, / O God, you will not despise" (NIV). David's sins had caught up with him. He was a broken man. God promises to meet us as he met David, who came to him acknowledging his great need.

God opposes the proud but gives grace to the humble. Pride is the greatest of all evils. It is our worst enemy and dies the slowest and hardest death. If we want to be blessed, we must first be broken. To be broken means to be shattered, to feel as if our entire world is falling apart, and as though our tears will never stop flowing. Our nation is slowly recovering from the worst financial crisis since the Great Depression. Life savings have been wiped out; retirement plans have been destroyed. Many are still searching for jobs. In this time of brokenness many of us will turn to God in a new way because there is nowhere else to turn.

Nothing feels blessed about being broken. In Jeremiah 18:2-6 we see a vivid description of brokenness. The potter is working at the wheel, and the clay has to be smashed on the potter's wheel and reshaped. The potter's purpose is not to destroy his work, but to make a perfect work—to shape and fashion something more beautiful and more functional.

Being broken means we are willing to submit our lives to the lordship of Jesus Christ. The broken person will find all the resources of heaven at his or her disposal. James 4:7 urges, "Submit yourselves . . . to God." When we submit, we yield ourselves totally to God. We surrender our lives and everything that is connected to us into the hands of God. The broken and contrite heart is easily molded by the hands of a gracious God. Samuel Chadwick wrote, "It is a wonder what God can do with a broken heart if He gets all the pieces." Let's give him all the pieces of our broken dreams, our broken hearts, and our broken lives, and we will be amazed at what he can do.

Choose to Open Yourself to God's Love

What is brokenness? It is not a feeling or an emotion. It requires a choice, an act of the will. True brokenness is an ongoing way of life. It is a lifestyle of working with God and asking, *What is the true condition of my heart and life?* And answering, *It is the shattering of my self-centeredness and the absolute surrender of my will to do God's will.* The word *contrite* means something that is crushed into small particles or ground into powder as a rock is pulverized. It is only with a contrite heart that we can humbly ask for God's help and receive God's love.

John Bunyan, the author of *Pilgrim's Progress*, wrote, "The best prayers are often more groans than words." I have reached that point many times in my life, when all I could do was cry out to God, "Please help me." Time after time all I could pray was that simple but heartfelt phrase of desperation until I experienced a marvelous breakthrough from God. When I earnestly said that simple prayer in complete brokenness and trust, God knew my concerns even better than I did.

God works in many ways to break our self-will. C. S. Lewis described his breaking process as he wrote, "When I invited Jesus into my life, I thought he was going to put up some wallpaper and hang a few pictures. But he started knocking out the walls and adding on rooms. I said, 'I was expecting a nice cottage.' But He said, 'I'm making a palace in which to live.'" This quotation was used by God to break the heart of Chuck Colson, the right arm for President Richard Nixon during the Watergate conspiracy.

Following his experience with Watergate, Chuck Colson's life was broken. He found himself in prison, having lost practically everything he once had. After his conversion, he wrote,

> I believe that most believers must go through a period of breaking as they come truly to know God's grace. Isn't that what our faith is about? We must know the wretchedness of our sinful state before we turn to the Lord for rescue. For many of us, God's mercy must be the severest sort that allows us to come to the end of our abilities—the end of the rope—in order to see our need for him. Certainly my life has been an example of God's severe mercy in breaking those he loves.

Chuck Colson had come to understand that **God is bigger than any problem that we encounter.**

* * * * *

Believing God Is Bigger than Any Problem

R. G. Le Tourneau went to church one Sunday morning during World War II with a big problem on his
mind: he was to design a huge earth-moving machine.
In that morning worship service during the time of
silent prayer, God revealed to him the design for this
piece of machinery. He quickly sketched it on the back
of his worship bulletin. As soon as the service was over,
he called an emergency meeting with all of his engineers
and showed them the diagram of what God had
revealed to him. The engineers were amazed because it
was exactly the design that they had been searching for
but had not been successful in discovering. Yes, God
will help us see things from his point of view.

Memorize This

There is no problem too big for God! I have mem-
orized that simple statement, and I repeat it daily. We
who tap into the vast resources of God's power take
God at face value. We trust him to do what he says he
will do. Our prayers are Christ centered, not problem
centered. When God says he will do something, we can
trust him totally. God delights to do impossible things
through improbable people to impart exceeding grace
to an undeserving recipient.

God does not lie. What he says, he will do. When he makes us a promise, we can count on it. When we pray, God's promises—not the severity or the size of the problem—must become our focus. Many times we start out praying about a serious problem with an attitude of faith, but over time we turn our prayers into worry sessions in which we tell God how upsetting the situation is to us. Then we try to bargain with him to tell him how faithful we have been, how good we have been, and how generous we have been. Bargaining with God will get us absolutely nowhere.

Keep Your Focus on God

It is so easy to end up totally absorbed in our problems rather than depend upon his grace and promises. When we look at God through the lens of our problems, God gets smaller and the problems get bigger. Focusing on the size of the problem rather than on God and the power of his promise is like looking through binoculars backward.

Some of us may have said, "I'm just not going to have enough money to support myself"; "My 401(k) has been destroyed"; or "My portfolio is practically down to nothing." Then we turn to Philippians 4:19 and find God's wonderful promise, "My God shall supply all your need according to his riches in glory" (KJV). Or maybe we've said, "I'm not sure I can hold on any longer. I'm at the end of my rope. I'm about ready to quit and throw in the towel." Then we read 2 Corinthians 12:9: "[God's] grace is sufficient for you, for power is made perfect in weakness." Or maybe we are going through a seemingly impossible situation. We cry out, "It is just too hard. I don't see any way out. I'm not going to make it." Then we turn in the Bible and find God's promise in Philippians 4:13: "I can do all things through Christ who strengthens me" (NKJV).

Or maybe the word *overwhelmed* describes our situation. Maybe we feel overwhelmed with all the problems, with all the stress, with all the things going wrong in our lives at a particular moment. We certainly do not want to go through all this by ourselves. We feel helpless and hopeless and terribly afraid and alone. Then God leads us to this promise: "I am with you always, even to the end of the age" (Matthew 28:20 NKJV).

Relax and Let Go!

Stress, worry, and anxiety block creativity and problem solving. Prayer has a way of relaxing our minds so that we can be more receptive to God's ideas and plans. Often big problems require longer periods of prayer and reflection; therefore, we need to set aside a day or an afternoon to get away and spend time alone with

God. I also try to have a place that I can go and not be disturbed by phones or other interruptions.

Many times after I have taken a walk or ridden around on our family ranch, God has helped me clear the cobwebs and made me more open and receptive to his insight and his guidance. Before I go to sleep, I pray and ask God to work through my subconscious mind for a solution to the problem. Many times I have been awakened in the middle of the night or early in the morning with a flash of insight or an idea that solved the problem. I've learned to keep a pen and notebook in the nightstand beside my bed so that I can record the idea. If I don't write it down immediately, I will forget it by morning.

People who really trust God and take seriously his promises experience an unbelievable adventure of faith. Each of us should ask, *What big problem do I need to bring to him today? What promise do I need to claim? How much power do I need to receive in order to make it through?* **How can I keep my mental and spiritual contact points clean so that God's power can operate in my life?**

* * * * *

Keeping Contact Points Clean so That God's Power Can Operate

One morning I tried to start my car, but it simply made a clicking sound. A good friend raised the hood and discovered that the contact points on the battery had become corroded. He carefully scraped away the corrosion and asked me to once again try to start the car. It immediately cranked. I've discovered that God's power can be blocked because of corrosion in our lives. Spiritual gunk gets around our contact points with God.

A lack of faith can be one corrosive hindrance to answered prayer and God's power. Many of us pray but never really expect God to answer. James 1:6-7 states, "He must ask in faith without any doubting, for the one who doubts is like the surf of the sea, driven and tossed by the wind. For that man ought not to expect that he will receive anything from the Lord" (NASB). Why waste time and effort praying if we really do not believe God is going to answer our prayers? We need to remember what Jesus said in Matthew 17:20: "If you have faith the size of a mustard seed, you will say to this mountain, 'Move from here to there,' and it will move." When we pray, we must really believe and expect God to answer our prayers.

A bit of spiritual gunk is to answered prayer as unconfessed sin. Unconfessed sin will cause a major disconnect and break the circuit between us and God, as the psalmist wrote, "If I regard wickedness in my heart, the Lord will not hear" (Psalm 66:18 NASB). Unconfessed sin destroys our relationship with God and breaks down the channel of power into our lives. I ask God to reveal to me anything that I am unwilling to give up or to confess as sin. There is no sin worth holding on to if it disables my prayer life and makes it ineffective and powerless.

A pastor's young son found a cigar and went to the alley to light it. His dad came along, and the young boy put the cigar behind his back. He tried to divert his dad's attention by pointing to a billboard announcing a circus that was coming to town. He asked, "Dad, can I go to the circus?" His dad wisely replied, "Son, you need to learn something in life. You don't ask for special favors when you have a smoldering disobedience behind your back!" Most of us have tried to divert God's attention from what we've done by pointing in another direction. First John 1:9 states, "If we confess our sins, He is faithful and just to forgive us our sins and to cleanse us from all unrighteousness" (NKJV). Keeping our mental and spiritual contact points clean is essential to effective prayer.

Another corrosive barrier is wrong motives—for example, our selfishness. James 4:3 states, "You ask and do not receive, because you ask with wrong motives, so that you may spend it on your pleasures" (NASB). How would we feel if our prayer requests were made public, displayed on a large billboard for everyone to

see? If my prayer is self-serving, with the primary moti-
vation to show off in front of others, it will not be
answered. We need to ask, *If this request is granted, will
it bring glory to God or to me? Will it advance his kingdom
or my own? Will it help others, or will it be selfish? What is
my real motive in praying this prayer?*

**One more corrosive barrier to answered prayer
is an unforgiving spirit.** Many people hold grudges,
resentments, and bitterness toward others. This is especially true for those who have hurt us or loved ones who
have betrayed us. In a 1979 *Guidepost* edition is the story
of Eugene, who lost several hundred dollars that he
loaned to a fellow worker. He grew bitter and miserable. One morning at church, while he was reciting the
Lord's Prayer, "Forgive us our debts, as we forgive our
debtors," something happened. The Lord spoke to his
heart: "Eugene, you, too, are a delinquent debtor to Me.
And your debt is immeasurably larger than any mone-
tary debt that someone owes you. But your account is
settled, forgiven. It took the death of My Son to do it.
Now just what did you want to tell Me about your
friend that owes you some money?" Over a period of
weeks Eugene began to change, and with the Lord's
help he forgave the man, and his prayer life came back
on stream. Nothing can hinder or block our prayer life
any more than the failure to forgive. An unforgiving

spirit is lethal both physically and spiritually. We must let go of that resentment and anger and, instead, forgive. I have been amazed at the peace that has come into my life when I have practiced forgiveness.

Any one of these barriers may keep God's power from flowing into our lives. We may be held back from God's power and goodness by resentment, evil thoughts and actions, or negative thinking. In such cases, our prayers can't get through to God for the simple reason they never got out of us. God's power, which tends to flow toward us, is blocked off, not because we do not desire this power, but because the mental barricades that we've created prevent it from getting into our personalities. When such thoughts and actions are removed, spiritual power will once again flow with a rush. Things will then be changed because we are changed.

Lord, Lead Me to Others on Your Team

When I pray for guidance, I ask God to lead me to other people who can be a part of his problem-solving team. I've learned that none of us is as smart as all of us. I pray for ideas or for him to lead me to a book or some other helpful resource that will provide additional insight on the issue. Having a collaborative team is much more effective in solving major problems than trying to do it all by myself.

I don't hesitate to hire experts who deal with my type of problem every day. It will be the best money that I ever spend. Several years ago I was involved in a property settlement that required having an expert attorney from Texas who had written the real estate code for the entire state. His expertise was very expensive, but it was worth every penny that I paid him. His insight into Texas law was invaluable in winning that part of the case.

I've always had a team or a small group of friends with whom I can share my problems. I can trust these people completely for prayer, for encouragement, and for godly counsel; in addition, they will tell me the truth regardless of how painful that may be. For many years I've been blessed to have a group of trusted men in my church who pray for me daily. I am so thankful that we were never meant to face our problems all alone. At just the right moment God will send into our lives the people we need to get us through our struggles as **we pray our way through every difficulty until there is a release or an answer.**

* * * * *

Praying through Difficulties until There Is Release

Many years ago I spoke at a church service, and afterward, an older woman came up to me and said, "Pat, when you pray with people, **make sure that they pray through.**" I didn't quite understand what she meant, but later it became obvious that she meant to pray until you get a release or an answer to the prayer. So many times we stop short in our prayer life. So many times we pray only for a brief time and then give up. Instead, we must visualize the prayer being answered and praise and thank God in advance for his answer. John Wesley, Methodism's founder, reminded us that "God does nothing but in answer to prayer."

We pray most effectively when we mentally picture God working in and through the problem in a specific way. We imagine that the person we are praying for is in one room and Jesus Christ is in the next room. We are the contact between the two. As we pray for someone, we connect that person's need with God's immense power. Vividly and specifically, we can see the need met in the other person's life. Prayerfully, we imagine how different that person's life will be when the prayer is answered. We agree to be a part of the answer to the prayer if necessary and to be used by the Lord to answer our prayer.

When I pray for someone, I bring the power of God to bear on that person's life and situation. Following the admonition in James 5:14-16, I cooperate with God, praying as though everything depends on him and working as though everything depends on me. I dare to get involved in that person's life, the crisis, or the situation. There's no need to waste my time praying for someone's life to be changed or problems to be solved unless I am willing to get involved.

Finally, we **must persevere**; praying with power involves continuing to pray until the answer comes or a release occurs. It involves paying the price—the price of time, energy, and emotional pain. If we are really burdened for someone and really feel what that person feels, we can't possibly stop praying until the problem is solved. Matthew Henry wrote, "When God is ready to pour out unusual mercies, He sets His people to praying." And so we **P.U.S.H.—Pray Until Something Happens.**

The true test of loyalty to our friends and family is proved in our willingness to lay down our lives for them in prayer. Our faithfulness to our friends can be measured by our consistency and our prayers for them. We must pray consistently for those we love. A former pastor of First United Methodist Church in Houston, Texas, visited an older woman in his congregation whose heart had been broken by a wayward son. She asked the pastor, "Why do you suppose God is keeping me here?" She paused for a moment before she answered her own question: "God is keeping me here to pray for my son!" How true for many of us.

E. M. Bounds once said, "What the world needs most are people who really pray. Not those who just talk about prayer or teach about it and try to explain it, but actually do it." Great prayers have the potential and power to change the world. Our challenge is to pray powerful prayers, to pray through our problems until we get a release or an answer. We step out in faith and trust God, who is the God of miracles, to do what he has promised. Through prayer, we fall deeply in love with the living God and allow him to use our lives to be channels of blessing and power to others in need.

An older Scotsman who was very ill was visited by his pastor. As the pastor sat down by the bed, he noticed another chair by the bedside. The pastor asked the Scotsman about the chair, and the man replied, "Years ago I had a hard time praying. One day I discussed the problem with my pastor. He told me not to worry about kneeling down, just sit down. He also said, 'Put a chair opposite you and imagine Jesus is in it and talk to him as you would your very best friend.'" The man added, "I've been doing it ever since." A short time after that visit the Scotsman's daughter called to tell the pastor that her father had died. She said, "I lay down for an hour or two because he seemed to be sleeping comfortably. When I went back to check on him, he was dead. He had not moved since I left him, except that his hand was on the empty chair at the side of the bed."

This story is a vivid reminder that in the midst of death and tribulation, God is there, and we can put our hands in his as well as in those of our loved ones. He says, "I am with you always, to the end of the age" (Matthew 28:20). We never walk alone. He is only a prayer away. He calls us to reach out to him, for this very moment he is reaching out to us.

Worth Remembering

- "You will seek me and find me when you seek me with all your heart" (Jeremiah 29:13 NIV).
- "I have been driven many times to my knees by the overwhelming conviction that I have nowhere else to go" (Abraham Lincoln).
- "It is a wonder what God can do with a broken heart if He gets all the pieces" (Samuel Chadwick).
- "We have to pray with our eyes on God, not on the difficulties or problems" (Oswald Chambers).
- "P.U.S.H.—Pray Until Something Happens. There is no problem too big for God."

Questions

1. Share a time when you felt close to God.
2. What kind of prayer life would you like to have with God? Are you willing to make an investment of your time and effort to grow closer to God?
3. How do people become broken? Where have you experienced brokenness in your life?
4. What is the biggest barrier to your prayer life?
5. What does it mean to pray until there is a release?

Power Connection

Lord, thank you for the wonderful privilege of developing an intimate relationship with you. What a privilege it is to bring everything to you in prayer. Help me persevere until there is a release or an answer. Amen.

CHAPTER THREE

Come Help or High Water

MATTHEW 14:30-31

But when [Peter] saw the wind, he was afraid and . . . cried out, "Lord, save me!" Immediately Jesus reached out his hand and caught him. (NIV)

My wife, Sheri, taught first-graders for thirty-two years in the same neighborhood in which she grew up. As a result, she taught many of her high school classmates' children. One year, she had her best friend's son, Brad, in her class. Brad's family had gone through a difficult divorce the previous year. Sheri had given Brad's mother a little book, *God's Promises*, to help her through this terrible experience. Brad had observed his mother reading, praying, and finding strength through the book.

When the school year began, Brad had difficulty with the weekly spelling tests. One Friday morning, Sheri asked her students to prepare for their spelling test. Brad immediately jumped up from his desk and ran to the back of the room to the coat rack and began digging through his backpack. Sheri followed him to see if he was trying to cheat on the test.

Needless to say, she was surprised to find Brad on his knees, kneeling and clutching a book to his chest, apparently praying! When she asked what he was doing, Brad replied, "You gave this book to my mother, and she reads and prays with it every day and says God will see us through our storms. I need God to see me through my spelling storm so I can make one hundred." Miracles do happen! Brad made one hundred on his test that day.

Because of the kind gesture from a friend, his mother's positive example, and his teacher's support, Brad learned a valuable lesson that day about preparing for the tests he will face in life and about trusting God's promises to see him through his storms. As Brad graduates this year from high school, he knows there have been many family members, friends, and other encouragers who have **helped him meet the high-water difficulties** of his young life. The lesson he learned that day in Sheri's first-grade classroom on trusting God with the help of those who care for him is one he will never forget.

Let's start attracting the people we need in our lives to make our dreams come true.

The human brain has an amazing capacity to attract what we want in life. But we must decide what we want before the brain can begin to figure out how to get it. **We must be willing** to dream big dreams. As soon as we commit to a big dream and really go after it, our creative minds will come up with a big idea to make it happen, and we will start attracting the people we need in our lives to make our dreams come true.

Come Help or High Water

I've always had a team or a small group of trusted friends with whom I can share my problems. I can trust them completely for prayer, for encouragement, and for godly counsel; in addition, they are men and women who will tell me the truth regardless of how painful that may be. This group prays for me daily. I can call any of them for prayer or counsel at any time. I am so thankful that we were never meant to face our problems all alone. At just the right moment God will send into our lives the people we need to get us through our struggles.

The characteristics of my team of friends, family, and colleagues are based on biblical principles:

- First, I need *truth tellers* on my team.
- Second, I need *problem solvers* on my team.

- Third, I need *wise and caring friends and family* on my team.
- Fourth, I need *spirit lifters* on my team.
- Finally, I need *generous and grateful givers* on my team.

* * * * *

Truth Tellers

Dr. Ken Blanchard reminds us in his book *Servant Leader*,

> We all need trusted truth-tellers, preferably those not directly impacted by what we do, who can help us keep on course. . . . **Having truth-tellers in your life is . . . probably your greatest opportunity for growth.** There are two main ways that growth takes place: When you're open to feedback from other people. When you're willing to disclose your vulnerabilities to other people.

God often targets the vulnerable area that needs to be broken, arranges the circumstances that lead to our breaking, and chooses even the tools that he uses to mold us in love. Jeremiah 18:6 describes the potter and the clay. Like clay in the hands of the potter, you and I are clay in God's hands. In his excellent book *The Wounded Healer*, Henri Nouwen writes, "All of our witness, all of our service, all of our good intentions for Christ will never be perceived as authentic until it comes from a heart that is wounded." We are challenged to let God transform our cancer, our broken relationships, our financial problems, our moral failures, and our weaknesses and let God transform them into something that he can use. We must be open and vulnerable to others about our lives so that we can be used as sources of healing and power in the lives of other broken people.

Then we can say with authenticity, "I know just how you feel." Who ministers to the alcoholic better than a reformed alcoholic? Or to the person with cancer than a person in remission? Or to someone whose marriage is failing than one who has gone through a divorce? Or to someone who has lost a loved one than one who has just experienced a similar loss? Or to someone facing impossible financial circumstances than one who has overcome financial crisis? God can transform our hearts into **truth-telling** channels of service and ministry to others. What does God want to do with our adversity, our suffering, our brokenness? He wants to take it, transform it, and use it as a healing channel of ministry to others.

A little boy went to a pet store to pick out his birthday present. He carefully looked at all the puppies and finally chose one that was without question the runt of the litter. The pet store owner said, "You don't want him. He will never be able to run and play." The little boy leaned over and pulled up his pants leg, revealing a leg brace. The little boy smiled and said, "I don't run too well either; he will need someone who understands." When we have gone through a major struggle, we are given a badge of authenticity. We have survived. We have truly been there. And we can speak that truth to others with love and understanding.

* * * * *

Problem Solvers

Problems motivate us to seek expert help or counsel in an area of difficulty. So many times when people come to my office to discuss their struggles, they begin by saying, "Never in a million years would I have imagined that I would have this problem (or be going through this struggle). I didn't know the first thing about overcoming or solving this problem (or struggle). I have been forced to learn everything that I could about it in order to survive."

When I am trying to solve a really big, tough problem, I need to learn as much as I possibly can about it. It may require learning new skills in order to deal with it. It may require doing extensive research and study or even going back to school. It may require consulting with an expert or hiring an expert for consultation and direction. My limited information base drastically begins to expand. I search everywhere for the things I need to know. I have an insatiable hunger or passion for learning that I didn't know before. Surely, being able to call on the **problem solvers** on my team makes this process much less stressful and much more likely to end in success.

In John 6:1-13 we see a huge problem: thousands of people are listening to Jesus, but there is not enough food to feed them when he is finished. Basically, there is a demand for which there is no apparent supply. The crucial point of the miracle comes when Jesus tells the disciples to **accept responsibility** for their problem, and they brainstorm for a solution. Their solutions were common reactions to huge challenges: procrastinating, passing the buck, and worrying about it. God tells us to do our part and he will do the rest.

As Matthew tells the story (14:13-21), the crowd included more than five thousand men, women, and children. When evening approached, the disciples went to Jesus and said, "This is a remote place and it is already getting late. Send them away so they can go and buy food for themselves." Then Jesus asked Philip to solve the problem. Philip got out his pocket calculator and figured quickly that eight months' wages would not buy enough bread for all the people to have even a single bite. The situation was impossible. Then Andrew brought the boy with five loaves and two fish to Jesus. At least it was a long shot. God insists we must live by faith and trust him to make the difference. We have to do what we can do. God says, "You do your part and I'll do the rest." The result: everyone had something to eat, and there were twelve baskets of leftovers. The loaves and fish used to feed the crowd that day teach us that problems are opportunities for people who are **problem solvers.**

God specializes in the humanly impossible. A miracle can happen only if the problem is bigger than the people. But we must do our part first. By including problem solvers on my team and trusting God, I allow him to take our little and do a lot with it. A miracle won't happen until we make the **commitment**. We expect God to do *for us* what he will only do *through us*.

* * * * *

Wise and Caring Friends and Family

At times in my life when I struggled, I learned how important my family and friends are to me and to my survival. I learned who my real friends are. When the water begins to rise, a lot of so-called fair-weather friends flee for safety. They don't want to be associated with us because they are afraid that what we are going through might accidentally get them wet too. But the true friends we discover will be people we can count on through good times and bad. They will be there when the chips are down. They will be some of God's greatest gifts to us when we are going through a tough time.

In Mark 2:1-10 four men had a **friend** who needed to have personal contact with Jesus Christ. The man was on a stretcher, but the crowds were so immense that his four friends could not get him to Jesus. Not to be deterred, however, they came up with a creative, imaginative plan. They climbed up on the roof of the house where Jesus was ministering, cut a hole in the roof, and lowered their friend so that Jesus could touch him. His life was forever changed. It never would have happened if his friends had not been daring and willing to think outside the box in order to help him.

I have learned that I must work at cultivating friendships with hopeful, positive, Spirit-filled people. I need to surround myself with people who lift me up and don't drag me down—people who will help me build my faith. Joining with friends in worship in a Christ-centered church encourages us and gives access to a positive message of faith and hope. Ruth Graham once said, "Worship and worry cannot live in the same heart. They are mutually exclusive."

Those of us who come from deeply caring families have a foundation of support for all the seasons of our lives. A soldier was once asked why he never seemed upset or worried in battle. His answer: "I don't come from a worrying family. My mom gave me a New Testament, and I've been carrying it ever since. That is where I get my confidence. I told her that she should give me one with a steel cover and maybe that would shield my heart from a bullet." She replied, "Son, there is steel in it and it ain't in the cover!" Yes, in the pages of the Bible there are steel, courage, confidence, faith, assurance, security and, of course, Jesus Christ. That is the secret of living with security in insecure times.

Two of the most formative years of my life were my first two years in college. I was on a football scholarship at Henderson County Junior College (Trinity Valley Community College presently) in Athens, Texas. I made many lifelong friends and had the privilege of playing football with and against some really great athletes. My freshman year I played on special teams and was a backup to the starting strong safety. My goal as a sophomore was to be a starter. I worked very hard in the off season and summer in order to earn a starting position. When the season began, I achieved my goal. All the hard work, sacrifice, and pain finally paid off.

In our second nonconference game against one of our major rivals, Kilgore Junior College, I was covering one of their receivers on a pass route. Their quarterback then threw the ball to the man I was covering. We both went up for the ball, and he caught it for a long gain. My coach immediately pulled me out of the game. There I sat for the remainder of the game—humiliated, disappointed, and defeated.

I went home for the weekend after the game. In her own insightful way my mother knew something was bothering me. She began to ask what was wrong. I dodged her questions the best I could for nearly the entire weekend until finally I told her about being benched for allowing an opponent to catch a long pass.

And then she asked a penetrating question: "Pat, have you allowed football to become your God? Have you put football in first place in your life? God is a jealous God, and he will not allow anyone or anything to be more important in our lives than our relationship to him." Her words hit me like a ton of bricks. Football had become an obsession—a god that I had come to worship.

I spent the remainder of the afternoon getting my priorities straight, especially my relationship with the Lord. I asked his forgiveness for putting football before him. Within the week I had regained my starting position on the team. Several weeks later we played Kilgore for the second time in a conference game. I tried my best to play for God's glory and not my own. Much to my shock and amazement, after the game was over and we had won, the coach gave me the outstanding defensive player award. I've never forgotten my mother's words. To this day I still ask myself: **Who or what is more important than my relationship to God? Who or what is number one in my life?** My mother set my feet on the right path many times. I shall always be grateful for her wisdom and her love.

* * * * *

Spirit Lifters

When I have gone through a major crisis, I have battled many negative emotions such as hurt, anger, resentment, guilt, fear, and an unforgiving spirit. I have learned that survivors find healthy channels such as talking, sharing, exercising, and crying to express and process these negative feelings. We don't bottle up our hurt feelings, nor do we complain and force our pain on others. Instead, we share in positive ways with the **spirit lifters** we discover in our lives.

A little girl's best friend was killed when she was hit by a car while she was riding her bike. The little girl asked her mother for permission to go over and express her sympathy to the mother of the child who was killed. After the little girl returned, her mother asked her, "Well, what did you say to her?" The girl replied, "I didn't say anything; I simply crawled up in her lap and helped her cry." Many times the best thing in such situations is not what we say, but what we do: simply be there with our tears of compassion and love. Tears are God's gift to all of us, allowing us to release our feelings in healthy ways.

When Jesus Christ arrived in Bethany and found that Lazarus, his close friend, had died, the Scriptures record a simple fact: "Jesus wept" (John 11:35 KJV). And so will we when someone we love dies. In his book *Windows of the Soul*, Ken Gire describes the value of tears: "The closest communion with God comes, I believe, through the sacrament of tears. Just as grapes are crushed to make wine and grain to make bread, so the elements of this sacrament come from the crushing experiences of life." When our tears come, instead of feeling ashamed for shedding them or apologizing for them, we can remember their value. We must not listen to those who say we shouldn't let our feelings out. Nothing is more ridiculous than the statement, "Real men don't cry." Nothing could be farther from the truth, especially when we remember that the greatest man who ever walked on earth cried at the death of a close friend. And as the little girl did, our friends cry with us.

As a little boy, I visited my grandmother. She had an old tea kettle with a flapper on it. When the water began to boil, the tea kettle whistled, and the flapper flapped back and forth. If someone had taken a welding torch and sealed the flapper, the steam would have caused the tea kettle eventually to explode instead of whistle. The same happens in our lives when we do not release the emotions that are built up in us.

Spirit lifters are often people who have survived a similar crisis and grown through the experience. We may know them personally, or we may have read about them. We can contact them, get to know them, and learn the life lessons that they share. There are wonderful people whose circumstances and crises are very similar to the ones that we are experiencing. We need them as a part of our team. Steve Ackerman, the first person who was a paraplegic to pedal around the world on a hand cycle, made this observation: "We give others the courage to do great things by our own example of doing great things."

I have observed that when an ice storm comes a lot of trees and limbs are broken under the weight of the ice. This is especially true for trees that are all alone. When trees are growing close together, their collective branches help support the weight of one another. When we go through tough times, we may mistakenly think, *I'm all alone—no one has suffered like I am suffering. I'm unique. I'm the only one in the whole world who has ever had this problem!* Nothing could be farther from the truth. This is one reason we need to become a part of a church. Our church provides a healing community. Survivors don't try to go it alone; they live in community. They realize they need the prayers, the love, the encouragement, the support, and the wisdom of others. They are not afraid or ashamed to ask others for help. They have people in their lives from whom they can learn and on whom they can lean.

In my first church in Grand Saline, Texas, I became close friends with a family there. John and Margaret were wonderful members of my church. One day Margaret went to her doctor for a routine checkup. The doctor discovered that she had leukemia and had only a short time to live. One Sunday after church I drove to the hospital to visit her. It was apparent that she didn't have long to live. She asked everyone in the room to leave but me. And then she weakly said something I will never forget. I leaned over so I could hear her whisper: "Pat, someday you are going to be a great man of God. Remain humble, depend totally on God, and he will use you in ways you cannot begin to imagine." After she said that, she smiled the most beautiful smile imaginable, closed her eyes, and went home to be with her Lord. I walked out of the room to tell her family that she had died. Her husband grabbed me and, with tears in his eyes, said, "I don't know how anyone can go through something like this without a wonderful church family."

I've often thought about what he said. How many people go through their storms and have no one to share the burden with, no one to lean on, no one who cares enough even to pray for them? When someone can truthfully say, "I know just how you feel," it means the world because they have gone through a similar experience, and it gives them credibility in helping us.

* * * * *

Generous and Grateful Givers

Generous and grateful givers use the knowledge and resources they have gained to help others. They have learned the secret and joy of giving. They have chosen to live generously. They are by intention generous people. They give of themselves. They freely share their influence for what is right and just in our world. They give of their money and time. They give of their knowledge. They use what they have learned to help others. They know how to channel their personal expertise, strength, knowledge, and hope to others who have taken some terrible hits. Not only do I need such people on my team, but I must also learn to be a generous and grateful giver for others.

We must put our pain and knowledge to work giving to others. Helping others makes us feel better about ourselves and those we help. If we have survived a major hit or setback, we can help others. There are many different ways that we can accomplish this purpose:

- Volunteer at a hospital or rehab center that deals with our particular problem.
- Give talks about our experience at civic groups and churches.
- Listen to people who are suffering similar problems.
- Write an article for a newspaper or magazine dealing with what we have learned, and include practical steps for helping others with the same issue.
- Volunteer to work on a crisis or help line.
- Work with other people in a support group focusing on the issue that God has given us grace to overcome.
- Organize a new ministry that deals with the setbacks that you experienced.

Following the death of his daughter Diane, Art Linkletter wrote,

> When you've had a major tragedy in your life, you are not going to be left unchanged. You are going to be changed. You have to choose. You can choose for the worse or you can choose for the better. You can try to find out if there is some way that you can make things better for other people, which I did in my own life.

In helping others work through their crises, I have learned much from them. I pray for God to show us those special people who have walked in our footsteps so that we can get to know them and learn from them. They can be valuable teachers for us as we go through our crises. What better examples do we have of committed, helping friendship than those many times that Jesus showed his loving care for his dear disciple Peter? In one instance, "when [Peter] saw the wind, he was afraid and . . . cried out, 'Lord, save me!' Immediately **Jesus reached out his hand and caught him**" (Matthew 14:30-31 NIV).

Celine Dion sings, "You gave me wings and made me fly." These beautiful words could well be a message that each one of us who has been through tough times can say specifically to another human being as well as to our very best friend, Jesus Christ.

Worth Remembering

- Having truth tellers in your life is one of your greatest opportunities for growth.
- We expect God to do for us what he will only do through us.
- "Worship and worry cannot live in the same heart. They are mutually exclusive" (Ruth Graham).
- "The closest communion with God comes, I believe, through the sacrament of tears. Just as grapes are crushed to make wine and grain to make bread, so the elements of this sacrament come from the crushing experiences of life" (Ken Gire).
- "We give others the courage to do great things by our own example of doing great things" (Steve Ackerman).
- "When you've had a major tragedy in your life, you are not going to be left unchanged . . . you have to choose. You can choose for the worse or you can choose for the better. You can try to find out if there is some way that you can make things better for other people" (Art Linkletter).

Questions

1. Who are the truth tellers in your life? Why would you classify them as truth tellers? Give examples.

2. What does God want you to do with your adversity or brokenness?
3. What steps do you take in solving a major problem or dealing with a huge crisis?
4. Are you working at cultivating friendships with hopeful, positive, Spirit-filled people? What are you doing to identify and to cultivate these important relationships?
5. Who would you like to be on your team of spirit lifters? Why would you choose to select them?
6. How has God used your experience with adversity and suffering to help another person?

Power Connection

Lord, thank you for what you are teaching me as I go through my crisis. Show me the special people you are calling me to help. May I be sensitive to your leadership as you arrange divine appointments each day in my life. Amen.

CHAPTER FOUR

Standing on the Solid Rock

PSALM 40:2

He set my feet on a rock / and gave me a firm place to stand. (NIV)

Experiencing struggles and solving problems are the very fabric of life for almost everyone. Most of us struggle to feel good about ourselves. We have times of insecurity, self-doubt, and low self-esteem. Worry is a stranger to none of us. Fears and frustrations seem to constantly assault us. We all have had periods of discouragement, disappointment, and feelings of depression. Every one of us has memories that haunt and unfulfilled dreams that hurt. What we really need to discover is **a *new* God for *old* struggles.**

We need a life-changing relationship with the true God of the Bible who **knows, cares, intervenes, and acts.** A God who **is present and powerful**, and who

makes things happen! What we all need today is a God who can transform the valley of human suffering. We were never meant to struggle alone. Most struggles in our lives come because we have painted ourselves into a corner of impossibility. We can't imagine that things will ever change. Our human efforts seem futile, with failure the only possible result. We do not have a choice about the problems that we will face in life, but we do have a choice about how we will respond when they come. We may respond with determination and fortitude, or we may just give up.

We should choose to **expect, anticipate, and welcome problems**. A person was asked this question: "Problems have a way of coloring life, don't they?" The person wisely replied, "Yes, but I get to choose the color." When problems pile up, we have a choice of how we will react to them. Let's face our problems instead of running from them. When David fought Goliath, the Scriptures read, "David ran quickly toward the battle line to meet the Philistine" (1 Samuel 17:48). David confronted his problem head-on.

We must welcome our problems as gifts from God. Dr. Lloyd Ogilvie writes, "The greatest problem we all share is the profound misunderstanding of the positive purpose of problems. Until we grapple with the gigantic problems, we will be helpless victims of our problems throughout our lives." We have a choice: Will we be victims or victors? In his book *The Road Less Traveled*, psychiatrist Scott Peck writes, "It is in this whole process of meeting and solving problems that life has its meaning." He goes on to say,

> Life doesn't have meaning unless we learn how to handle our problems. Problems are the cutting edge that distinguishes between success and failure. Problems call forth our courage and our wisdom; indeed they make our courage and wisdom. It is only because of problems that we grow mentally and spiritually. It is through the process of confronting and resolving problems that we learn.

Standing on the Solid Rock

We are successful in facing our problems with courage and fortitude if we **stand on the solid rock** of these principles:

- First, problems are the starting point of great dreams.
- Second, goals are dreams in chunks of reality.
- Third, action plans are the road maps for achieving our goals.
- Fourth, fortitude and courage are essential to completing action plans.

- Finally, God will not forsake us nor will he allow us to simply drift into life's storms.

* * * * *

Problems Are the Starting Point of Great Dreams

Why not address our problems as if we are taking the most important journey that we will ever experience? By treating the resolution of our problems as the focus of our hopes and dreams, we can create a map to reach our goals. Theodore Roosevelt suggested that a goal is the execution of a dream. A goal is a dream turned into achievable chunks of reality. Goals give us purpose and direction. If we don't know where we are going, how do we expect to get there? Ask yourself, *Specifically, what would I like for my life to be like when my problems are resolved?*

* * * * *

Goals Are Dreams in Chunks of Reality

One of the best ways to begin setting goals is to ask God to direct our goal setting. In Jeremiah 29:11 we read, " 'For I know the plans I have for you,' declares the LORD, 'plans to prosper you and not to harm you, plans to give you hope and a future' " (NIV). What a wonderful promise! God promises that he already has plans and goals for our lives. He knows us better than anyone else knows us. He has specific things in his mind and heart that he wants us to achieve and to do for him. Therefore, we begin our goal setting by asking God what his desires are for us. We must

- be specific.
- employ prayer and meditation.
- listen carefully to what God may speak to our hearts.
- never underestimate what God wants to do for us and in and through us.

As we open our Bibles and begin reading the passages related to our goals, God seems to be leading us. We ask him, "What do you want me to do with my life?" We fast, pray, and write down what God speaks to our hearts.

Our goals should be **S.M.A.R.T.**, that is, **specific, measurable, attainable, realistic, and timely.** We must never set goals that we can reach on our own strength and ability. Rather, we must set goals that stretch us, challenge us, and require us to get outside our comfort zone and trust God in a new way. Jim Rohn says, "You want to set a big enough goal so that in achieving it you become someone worth becoming."

Several years ago a survey was taken of students in the Harvard Business School. Eighty-four percent of the students had no goals for their lives. Thirteen percent had goals but had never written them down. Only 3 percent had goals and plans for achieving them. That 3 percent earned ten times more than the other 97 percent combined. J. C. Penney once said, "Give me a store clerk with a goal, and I will give you a man who will make history. Give me a man without a goal, and I will give you a store clerk."

If we are to be like the 3 percent in the Harvard study or the person who will make history, we must commit ourselves to working to achieve our goals. We will resolve our problems and achieve our dreams if we

- clearly define our goals in all areas of our lives and write them out.
- devise a strategy for achieving them.
- plan the problem areas—face up to the obstacles that we are going to encounter.
- set a time frame for the accomplishment of our goals.

We must not fill in our goals without God's input and expect him to make them come true. Four great questions frame our goal setting:

1. Why is this important to **you**, Lord?
2. Does this fit **your** plan for my life?
3. Is this goal in line with the **Bible**, or does it in any way contradict the teachings of the Scriptures?
4. How might the accomplishments of the goals **bless others**?

For many years in the early part of January I set my goals and then put them before the Lord and asked him to bless them and make them come true. As I've grown in wisdom and in years, I've learned to sit with a blank sheet of paper and ask God what *he* wants rather than what *I* want. The change has been dramatic in my life as I have begun to ask God to be the one setting the goals.

* * * * *

Action Plans Are the Road Maps for Achieving Our Goals

Peter Drucker stated, "We greatly overestimate what we can do in one year, but we greatly underestimate what is possible for us to do in five years." To maintain steady progress on the road toward success, we must develop a course of action for achieving our goals and a deadline for their achievement. That action plan should include *deciding* what we need to do first and what we need to do later and *setting the priority* for each action step. We must determine to do something every day on our action plan. In other words, we will **plan our work and then work our plan.** Napoleon Hill once said, "Every well-built house started with a definite plan in the form of a blueprint." We should remember this simple formula for success: **proper prior planning prevents poor performance.**

Each day comes to us as a gracious gift from our heavenly Father. What we do with it is our gift to him. An older man was building a log cabin all by himself. One of his friends asked, "Isn't that a big undertaking for a man your age?" The man smiled and replied, "It would be if I thought of chopping all the trees down, laying the foundation, erecting the walls, putting on the roof, and building the fireplace all by myself. That would exhaust and overwhelm me. But it isn't hard to cut down one tree a day." If we give our best every day and trust God for the rest, the future will take care of itself. We can have the most life-changing, most challenging goals possible, but if we don't turn them into a course of action to implement our plan, our goal will remain just that—a goal—and we will never solve our problems or reach our dreams.

* * * * *

Fortitude and Courage Are Essential to Completing Action Plans

We must be willing to pay the price to achieve our goals. Success is the intersection where dreams and hard work meet. If we work hard and love our work, we can do anything that we honestly aspire to. There are no shortcuts to success. We can succeed only with hard work, application, dedication, self-discipline, and sacrifice. It takes hard work and courage to be a successful spouse, parent, businessperson, or faithful follower of Jesus Christ.

Successful people are willing to do the things that other people will not do. What can we do today to take our lives to the next level? We can develop a strong work ethic. The difference between champions and contenders is not necessarily talent or ability. The gold medal usually goes to the one who has worked the hardest, the smartest, and the longest to achieve the goal. General Colin Powell commented about this point: "A dream doesn't become reality through magic; it takes sweat, determination, and hard work." Proverbs 14:23 states, "All hard work brings a profit, / but mere talk leads only to poverty" (NIV). The difference between where we are and where we want to be is not measured in miles. It is measured in hard work. This does not mean becoming obsessed with succeeding or becoming a workaholic. People who become obsessed with their work burn out quickly. These individuals tragically lose balance in their lives. Rest, relaxation, and recreation are essential to living a healthy, wholesome, well-balanced life.

In the movie *The Pursuit of Happyness*, Will Smith plays a homeless father who cares greatly about his son and wants to provide for him. This movie is a true story about Chris Gardner, who transformed his life from being a homeless father to becoming an outstanding stockbroker. The movie depicts his passion and his dream from being penniless to being able to provide for the son he literally worships. The movie shares all of his ups and downs and challenges and sacrifices that he experiences in order to ultimately reach his goal of landing an internship with Dean Witter & Company. Gardner's story is a powerful illustration of how fortitude and courage, together with goal setting, can make our dreams become reality.

Thomas Edison once said, "If my life had been made up of eight-hour days, I don't believe I could have accomplished a great deal." He went on to say, "Opportunity is missed by most people because it is dressed in overalls and looks like work." There is nothing more satisfying than to set a goal, work, and sacrifice until that goal becomes reality. It is the greatest builder of self-confidence and self-esteem that I know. I ask you, my reader:

- What is your dream?
- What is your goal?
- What is God asking you to achieve or to become?

Let's Go for It!

Most of us want to use our lives to raise our minds and spirits to new levels. It is what every parent wants to do for his or her child. It is exactly what every leader ultimately wants to do for his or her organization. Moving to the next level can be done only when we encounter and conquer the obstacle that is in our way. It is amazing how many problems have the unique power to inspire exceptional effort and refocus our priorities; to hone our character and unleash some of the most powerful forces imaginable within us. If we eliminate problems and struggles, we miss out on life's deepest, richest, highest gifts and its most powerful lessons. The more we struggle to escape our problems, the less we become.

In his book *The Adversity Quotient*, Dr. Paul Stoltz talks about three kinds of people. The first group is **divers or quitters**; they make up approximately 20 percent of the population. They simply give up as they begin to climb the mountain or obstacle that they face. As things get tough, they throw in the towel. In other words, they take a dive. Words such as *can't*, *won't*, and *impossible* fill the vocabulary of this group.

The second group is **survivors or campers**; they make up about 75 percent of the population. They work hard. They apply themselves, and they pay their dues and do what it takes to reach a certain level. Then they plant their tent stakes and settle for the current elevation. "This is good enough," they say. "This is as far as I want to go. Things could be worse, and I am thankful that I am where I am today."

The third group is **thrivers or climbers; people within this** rare breed continue to learn, grow, strive, and improve until they have reached their full potential. Approximately 5 percent of the population is included in this group. Life for them is filled with challenges and possibilities. They can truly say, "I gave it my all. Let's just do it! The time to act is now!" Climbers strive toward results, and their language reflects their direction. Their favorite scriptural passage is Philippians 4:13: "I can do all things through Christ who strengthens me" (NKJV).

The differences among the three are what they do with their problems and their struggles. Divers abandon the climb when the going gets tough. Survivors hunker down. Thrivers take on new challenges of learning, growing, striving, and proving and making a difference until their final breath.

The English word *character* comes from a Greek word that means "an engraving tool, a die for stamping an image." **Our problems and struggles can become God's tools for engraving his image on our character.** If affliction refines some, it consumes others. The same sun that melts ice hardens clay. The choice is ours. "Why has God made me like this?" a woman with a disability asked her pastor. Wisely, he replied, "God has not made you. He is making you." The Master Craftsman is our loving heavenly Father. We are the raw materials. Suffering and our struggles are the tools, and Christian character is the process.

Many years ago when I was going through a particularly painful struggle, I was reminded that there was a purpose for my suffering. For the life of me, in the midst of the experience, I couldn't make any sense of my experience. I turned to God, but he didn't seem to make much sense either. But as I have grown, my understanding of the experience has deepened. There was a purpose in my struggle, even though I may never on this side of eternity completely understand. I've come to believe that it is all right to question, search, and explore to find a purpose. It is all right not to completely understand that purpose and simply to trust God, who has the big picture for my life. I don't have to have all the answers to my questions, nor do I need to understand everything completely. But I do believe absolutely these words in Romans 8:28: "That in all things God works for the good of those who love him, who have been called according to his purpose" (NIV). Many times in my life, I've desperately clung to this promise. It has been a spiritual life preserver when I have almost drowned in a sea of doubt, despair, and discouragement.

God Will Not Forsake Us, Nor Will He Allow Us to Simply Drift into Life's Storms

J. C. Penney, in his autobiography, *Fifty Years with the Golden Rule*, tells of being in a sanatorium one night when he thought he was dying. He was going through a major business downturn and was at the point of losing everything that he had worked his entire lifetime to earn. He wrote several letters, knowing that this was going to be his last night on earth. He went to bed that evening certain that he would not be alive the next morning. When morning came, he was shocked to discover he was still alive. He got up, and as he was walking down the hall, he heard some people singing, "Be not dismayed whate'er betide. God will take care of you." There were only a few people who had come for an early morning chapel service, so he slipped in and sat in the back. Quietly, someone read from the Bible and then led in prayer. Mr. Penney spontaneously said, "Lord, I can do nothing. Will you take care of me?" He wrote, "In the next few minutes something happened to me . . . it was a miracle." He later referred to that single experience as the moment when the Lord saved his life as well as his business.

So often our immediate reaction to a problem is alarm, fear, panic, and anger. We frantically ask, *What am I going to do?* When panic and fear set in, creativity and faith dry up. When problems pile up, we need the Lord's power and presence. He uses our problem to call us to a deeper relationship with him.

When Joshua received his marching orders from the Lord to lead the people of Israel into the promised land, he immediately was confronted with his insecurities, fears, and inadequacies. The Lord knew his human tendency was to focus on the impossible task and overlook God's unbelievable resources. God spoke to Joshua and reassured him: "I will give you every place where you set your foot, as I promised Moses. . . . No one will be able to stand up against you all the days of your life. As I was with Moses, so I will be with you; I will never leave you nor forsake you" (Joshua 1:3-5 NIV). What a great source of strength!

Then God gave Joshua a personal pep talk, reassuring him of the victory to come: "Be strong and courageous, because you will lead these people to inherit the land I swore to their forefathers to give them. Be strong and very courageous. Be careful to obey all the law my servant Moses gave you" (Joshua 1:6-7 NIV). As long as you keep your eyes on the Lord and his promises, you will be able to move forward with confidence and courage, knowing the Lord will be with you wherever you go.

We need to hear the same pep talk that God gave to Joshua. We must turn our eyes away from our problems and place those problems before the Lord. Tom Peters and Robert Waterman in their book *In Search of Excellence* make the point that a laboratory may produce solutions, but it doesn't make the solutions work: "You have to take your solutions out of the laboratory and introduce them to the problem."

George Washington Carver was a brilliant agriculture chemist and innovator. He did extensive research and promotion of alternative crops in order to replace the soil-depleting king of the South—cotton. He worked tirelessly to find ways that peanuts, soybeans, pecans, and sweet potatoes could be used to improve the quality of life in the South.

In 1921, he was asked to appear as an expert witness before the Ways and Means Committee in the United States House of Representatives. He explained to the committee the wide range of ways that the peanut could be utilized. At the end of his address the chairman asked, "Dr. Carver, how did you learn all of these things?"

Dr. Carver answered, "From an old book."

"What book?"

Dr. Carver replied, "The Bible."

The chairman inquired, "Does the Bible tell about peanuts?"

"No, sir," Dr. Carver replied, "but it tells about the God who made the peanut. I asked Him to show me what to do with the peanut, and He did it!"

Once God gives us the insight, the idea, or the solution to our problem, we must be obedient in carrying it out under his direction. We must make the decision confidently and without delay, knowing that God is with us. Obedience is the key for spiritual insight and knowledge. It releases the power and insight for future problem solving. Our present difficulties are preparation for trusting God in the future. We can be certain that new problems will come. We can be just as certain that God's grace and power will always be with us. What we **do with** our problems is far more important than what our problems **do to** us. No problem leaves us

where it found us. If we are obedient, our problems lead
us to God.

It is virtually impossible to really start living until we
break the worry habit, which is fed by our problems.
Worry and fear have reached epidemic proportions in
our country during the most recent recession. In an
MSN Money article columnist M. P. Dunleavey pointed
out the circumstances that many people are struggling
with today:

> You're worried about money—or even your job. You're
> worried about your spouse's job, whether you should
> refinance your home or what you'll do if the economy
> gets worse. Maybe the onslaught of dire predictions
> from the media is fraying your nerves. (Thank you, Mr.
> Buffett, for that inspiring image of our economy jack-
> knifing off a cliff.) Whatever the source, it's tough to
> escape a mounting sense of financial dread.

What can we do to make it through this storm? I sug-
gest a proactive approach of learning how to break the
worry habit. When we worry, we imagine things we fear
actually becoming reality. If our worries dominate our
minds long enough, they will also affect our actions. Just
as positive thinking and living tend to bring about desir-
able events, sooner or later negative thinking tends to
create conditions in which the unpleasant things that
we worried about have a better chance of coming to

pass. Worry is the interest paid on trouble before it comes due. In Job 3:25 we read, "The thing which I greatly feared is come upon me" (KJV). In Job's life, the things that he had feared and worried about finally came to pass because his mind was like a magnet attracting the very things he dreaded.

We "what if" ourselves to death. What if the stock market doesn't turn around? What if I lose my job? What if I get cancer? What if I can't retire? What if I lose my retirement savings? What if I get sick and can't take care of myself? Ninety percent of the things that we worry about never occur. We are like Mark Twain, who said, "I've been through some terrible things in my life, some of which actually happened."

We need to empty our minds of our worries and anxieties. Everywhere we look there are a lot of people who are anxious, uptight, and stressed out. Their minds are filled with negative, fear-filled thoughts. Many years ago Rabbi Joshua Liebman wrote *Peace of Mind*. He was overwhelmed with the number of people seeking his help, so much so that he died at the age of forty-one within three years of the publication of his best-selling book. He died trying to deal with the heavy burden of so many people's problems. He wrote, "I am appalled at the multitude of people who have never learned how to empty their minds."

Empty your mind. What a powerful, creative concept! Worries, concerns, and anxiety can fill our minds to capacity. Wouldn't it be wonderful if we could clear out our minds just like we clean out our storage rooms, garages, closets, or wastebaskets? Let's use visualization and symbolism to empty our minds as J. Arthur Rank did. Rank, an early pioneer of the film industry in Great Britain, founded what he referred to as the Wednesday Afternoon Worry Club. Each week he wrote on a piece of paper all of his worries. He put the paper in the Wednesday afternoon worry box. The following Wednesday he opened the box and discovered that only one-third of the items were still worth worrying about.

A friend in a class I was teaching shared how she dealt with her worries. She said she visualized Jesus Christ standing with a basket in front of him. She prayerfully wrote down all the things that she was worried about and placed them in the basket. Then she kneeled, and he placed his hands on her head and blessed her. Thus, she surrendered her worries in a very practical way. She smiled as she acknowledged that she was often tempted to return to take back her concerns.

For many years I have gone into our sanctuary and knelt at the altar. There is a specific place that I always kneel and, one by one, place my worries on the altar. There has been a tremendous release when I let go and let God. It is amazing how God gives a spiritual uplift and encouragement when I kneel before him, pray, and place those cares and concerns on the altar. My biggest problem is fighting the urge to sneak back in and take them off the altar and carry them home with me. Each of us can develop our own way of taking positive action against our worries.

We need to **replace worry with work**. Psalm 37:3 suggests that we try work as a remedy for our worries: "Trust in the LORD, and do good." Robert Frost once said, "The reason more people die from worry than from work, is that more people worry than work!" Physical labor is a great antidote to anxiety. How many times have we seen six men standing around a hole and one man down in the hole digging with a shovel? The situation reminds me of the quotation, "The man who leans on a shovel cannot expect to lean on God."

Focusing our attention on our work helps our minds be occupied, and there is no time to worry. Work is proactive; worry is reactive. Instead of sitting around worrying about what we might have lost or what we are going through, let's get to work and make it back. God is a God of restoration. Work will take our minds off our worries and channel our energy in a productive way. If we once made it, we can make it again. So let's get back to work and quit wallowing in self-pity.

We need to **find positive, creative channels for our anxious and worrisome thoughts**. With God's help we can change any destructive mental habit. We can work at saying something positive about everything that we have been thinking of as negative. We won't say, "I'll never be able to do that. I can't make a comeback." Instead, we will affirm, with God's help: "I can make a comeback from my setbacks." We will remember Philippians 4:13: "I can do all things through Christ who strengthens me" (NKJV).

We need to **work at keeping ourselves in shape, mentally and physically**. During a very stressful time that lasted over a number of years, I think I wore out at least three exercise machines at the fitness center! Seriously, it was one of the greatest ways to get all the negative emotions and energy out of my mind and my body. I worked out so hard that when I stopped, I was physically exhausted. Exercising was a wonderful stress reliever. To this day I work out consistently, primarily as a way to release stress. Resting and relaxing, coupled with eating a proper diet of healthy, enriching food, are extremely important in dealing with the worry habit. In addition to feeding our bodies, feeding our minds by reading positive, uplifting material, especially the Bible, supplements our faith and diminishes our worries.

I once went to my doctor to seek his help because I was so uptight. I will never forget what this gracious man did. He took out his prescription pad and wrote these words on it: "Lord, help me to remember that nothing is going to happen to me today that you and I together can't handle." That was the best prescription I have ever had in my life. From that moment on my life has been greatly changed by that simple sentence written by my doctor.

We get into serious trouble when we try to handle tomorrow's problems on today's grace. His grace will be totally sufficient for everything that we face today. We can trust and rely on God's provision and providence because he cares for us. So many times he says to me: "Just trust me!" When I do, my life is radically changed. When I don't, my life is miserable. Let us trust and rely on him. **He asks us: "Do you really believe? If so, then act like it!"**

Worth Remembering

- "You want to set a big enough goal so that in achieving it you become someone worth becoming" (Jim Rohn).
- "We greatly overestimate what we can do in one year, but we greatly underestimate what is possible for us to do in five years" (Peter Drucker).
- "A dream doesn't become a reality through magic; it takes sweat, determination, and hard work" (General Colin Powell).

- Our problems and struggles can become God's tools for engraving his image on our character.
- Worry is the interest paid on trouble before it comes due.
- "I've been through some terrible things in my life, some of which actually happened" (Mark Twain).
- We get into serious trouble when we try to handle tomorrow's problems on today's grace.

Questions

1. What do you desire your life to be like when you get through this time of testing?
2. What does God want you to do with your life?
3. What price are you willing to pay in order for your dream to become a reality?
4. Are you a quitter, a survivor, or a thriver? Which would you like to become?
5. How has your storm helped shape you into the person you are today?
6. What do you worry about? What steps can you take to break the worry habit?
7. What is your biggest obstacle to really trusting God?
8. What can you do to overcome it?

Power Connection

Lord, help me remember that nothing is going to happen to me today that you and I together can't handle. Help me completely trust you. Thank you for your grace, guidance, strength, and companionship. Thank you for being there with me each step of the way. Amen.

CHAPTER FIVE

Seeing through the Eye of the Storm

HEBREWS 12:1

*And let us run with perseverance the race
marked out for us. (NIV)*

What is the source of the spiritual stamina and muscle for our lives? It comes from the struggles, the problems, and the storms that we face. Our struggles are like those of the moth as it perseveres to leave its cocoon. God uses our struggles to develop our spiritual muscles. The caterpillar spins a safe outer shell, or cocoon. As metamorphosis begins to take place within, the caterpillar is amazingly transformed. The struggle to emerge from the cocoon is essential for developing the muscle system of the moth's body and pushing the body fluids into the wings to expand them. If anyone or anything attempts to help it prematurely escape from the cocoon, the intervention will cost the maturing moth its life.

Unlike the caterpillar, most of us shrink from the challenges we face, and we fail to persevere. We want God somehow miraculously to snip the cocoon of our struggles and get us out of the messes we are in. We often find ourselves asking God to release us, "Just get me out of this mess." The Christian life is one of continuous growth and struggle. We all want to grow, but we don't want to pay the price for it. The old locker room phrase, "No pain, no gain," is true in life. **God whispers to us in our storms.** He knows we need to grow, and he provides the perfect challenge, the perfect struggle, and the perfect problem to help us become our best for him. Douglas Malloch once said, "Good timber does not grow with ease; the stronger the wind, the stronger the trees." The winds of our personal storms provide the very resistance necessary to develop us into the strong men and women God wants us to become.

President Calvin Coolidge gave us a lesson about the value of persistence:

> Nothing in the world can take the place of persistence. Talent will not; nothing is more common than unsuccessful men with talent. Genius will not; unrewarded genius is almost a proverb. Education will not; the world is full of educated derelicts. **Persistence and determination alone are overwhelmingly powerful.**

Let's consider the following very different cases:

- Fifteen publishers and thirty agents turned down John Grisham's first novel, *A Time to Kill.* More than sixty million copies of his novels are now in print.
- Every major studio in Hollywood rejected George Lucas's movie *Star Wars* until 20th Century Fox agreed to produce it. It became one of the top-grossing motion pictures of all time.
- Albert Einstein's math teacher labeled him, "Never will amount to much." And yet he did not allow that unflattering nickname to slow him down or stop him from making some of the greatest contributions in human history.

Grisham, Lucas, and Einstein were successful and made valuable contributions to art, culture, and science because they chose to persevere.

If we are to persevere to become the changed people that God wants us to be, we can take specific steps as we work through the storms in our lives. We must

- look forward, not backward.
- recognize that struggles reveal and refine our true character.
- learn to trust and rely unconditionally on God.

- imagine how Jesus Christ might have dealt with the problem in his earthly ministry.
- expectantly and prayerfully imagine and anticipate the way God will transform the problem into a possibility.
- look beyond the problem.

As we move through the eye of our storms, we can take these steps to persevere in the struggles that those storms may bring.

* * * * *

Look Forward

Yesterday is gone. We are not our past, though it is an excuse many people use when they attempt to avoid personal responsibility for their failures. So many times I have heard people say, "I can't do that. I had a bad childhood (or I was born across the tracks)." Or, "I've been hurt in the past. Therefore I can't do what I am asked to achieve." When I am going through a difficult time, I always believe that better times are just around the corner. I have learned that a positive, faith-filled hope for the future is essential in surviving in a difficult world. All of us are influenced by the past, but the past does not have to control the future unless we choose to allow it. I have seen many successful people make wonderful contributions that have made our world a better place in which to live. These people have gone through exactly the same set of difficult, if not impossible, circumstances that caused someone else to give up. We must decide today not to let our negative past control us but to be controlled by the future that God has in store for us.

We cannot blame the past. Rather, we must learn from it! I have adopted this motto for my life:

Learn from the Past, Live in the Present, and Look Forward to the Future

We need to focus on the present and work each day on our present goals. Let's look at our past and turn it into something positive. Paul learned a valuable lesson when he wrote in Philippians 3:13-14, "Forgetting those things which are behind, and reaching forth unto those things which are before, I press toward the mark" (KJV). Paul had a past that could have disabled anyone. He was instrumental in destroying the lives of many innocent people as he persecuted the followers of Jesus Christ. Once his life was changed, he continued to battle his past mistakes and failures, as all of us do. But there came a point in his life when God enabled him to release his past and move forward to an exciting new future. Is that where we are at this particular moment?

Perhaps we need to ask God to help us forget our past and move forward each day with his help to a fantastic new future that has unbelievable possibilities in store for us.

Recognize That Struggles Reveal and Refine Our True Character

Circumstances do not make us what we are; they reveal what we are. We are like tea bags: only when the water gets hot do we show our true colors. It is easy to present our best side when we are rested and not under the gun. When we are under pressure, exhausted, and sick, and things are unraveling in our lives, the real person is squeezed out. Reputation is what others think of us. Character is what we really are when no one is looking.

At a funeral the preacher talked about what a wonderful man the deceased was. Finally, after hearing a long list of superlatives, the widow of the man whispered to her little boy, "Go look in the casket and see who that man was. It certainly can't be your dad." Whatever else people may have, they have nothing without character. In *Becoming a Person of Influence*, Dr. John Maxwell states, "Reputation is what men say about you on your tombstone; character is what the angels say about you before the throne of God."

Suffering and adversities help us become more sensitive to others who are going through difficult times. Napoleon Hill, the author of the classic *Think and Grow Rich*, writes, "Every adversity, every failure, and every heartbreak carry with them the seeds of an equivalent or greater benefit." God prepares us for what he has prepared for us. Just as products aren't used until they are tested, so it is with us in serving God. We must become "wounded healers" before we can be greatly used by God.

Brokenness usually precedes blessing. The most painful and difficult times in my life have been those times when I literally felt broken, hurting so intensely that I thought I would never heal. Old habits, old desires, old patterns of reacting and relating are not easily changed. This process is painful and difficult, but it is essential if we are ever going to be used mightily by God. Think about an expensive thoroughbred colt. Before the colt can be ridden, it must be broken. The breaking process is difficult but absolutely essential if the animal is ever to be productive and to be used for its intended purpose. We must learn some lessons before we will be used. Brokenness brings us to a place where we say, "All that matters is God and his presence in my life." When we are going through tough times, we often pray, "What do you want me to do, say, and be today in order to bring you glory?" God always chooses to break a potential leader, often in the area of his or her greatest strength, before he uses that leader greatly.

Learn to Trust and Rely Unconditionally on God

During difficult times, we may feel that we have somehow been singled out or targeted for a particular adversity or problem. Learning to trust and rely unconditionally on God is the key to triumphant living. Two words have helped me cope during difficult times: *accept* and *trust*. That is, accept the mystery of hardships, sufferings, misfortune, and mistreatment. I must not try to understand it, just accept it.

Charlie Brown was carefully building a castle on the beach. Standing back to admire his work, he and his creation were soon engulfed by a downpour, which leveled the castle. Looking at the smooth place where his artwork once stood, he said, "There must be a lesson here. But I just don't know what it is." I totally agree with Charlie. So many times in life I do not understand, but I have learned in my own time of doubting, when my castles or dreams seem to be washed away, simply to trust God.

Many times Jesus Christ would ask those with whom he came in contact, "What do you want me to do for you?" As told in Mark 10:46-52, when word came to

Bartimaeus that Jesus Christ was entering his community, hope began to spring within this blind beggar's heart and soul: *Could Jesus Christ heal me?* Bartimaeus began to shout, "Jesus, Son of David, have mercy on me!" Finally Jesus stopped and asked this man one simple question: "What do you want me to do for you?" Bartimaeus replied, "Let me see again." He knew exactly what he wanted, and when the opportunity came, he asked Jesus for help. Bartimaeus let go of his pride and humbly but strongly asked to be able to see once again.

Too many people are too proud to ask for help. It is extremely difficult to humble ourselves and ask for help. Pride so many times gets in the way of receiving the very help that God wants to give us. It is very difficult to admit that we cannot solve our own problems. It's hard to ask someone to help when that situation is beyond our capabilities and beyond our control. But each of us needs to ask: *What do I spend much of my waking hours struggling to solve or to fix? What awakens me in the middle of the night? What do I pray about more than any other single issue? When I am with a close friend, what issues do I share or request prayer for?*

As a pastor counseling people with major problems, I've learned that people need to practice *triage*, a plan developed in World War I by doctors and nurses to more efficiently care for those wounded on the battle-field. The first group of soldiers was going to die regardless of what could be done, and they were placed in one section. The second group, if left unattended, would get well without a great deal of medical attention. They were placed in a totally different group. The third group required immediate medical attention, or the soldiers would die. These became the patients with the most urgent needs. Likewise, we have to determine the problem that is our top priority.

By clearly defining our biggest struggle and then focusing on it, we are able to understand the real cause of the problem. These questions can help us in that process: *What role did I play in causing the problem? How can I define the problem? Am I focusing on multiple problems?* Many times I have felt like Custer at Little Bighorn, seeing the Indians as they kept coming over the hill. It is very difficult to work on more than one big problem at a time. We can't do everything, but we can identify the one most important problem and persevere until we solve it.

Imagine How Jesus Christ Might Have Dealt with the Problem in His Earthly Ministry

It is helpful to reread the Gospels and see how Jesus Christ dealt with people and the problems they faced.

- **First, What Did He Say?**

He spoke words of comfort. For example, he said, "Let not your hearts be troubled; believe in God, believe also in me. In my Father's house are many rooms; if it were not so, would I have told you that I go to prepare a place for you?" (John 14:1-2 RSV). Across two thousand years, these words have given so many people wonderful comfort and assurance at the death of a loved one.

He gave wise counsel and direction. A Samaritan woman came to the well to draw water, and there Jesus Christ met her and gave her guidance and direction for her life. He shared the possibility that she could find living water, a living relationship that would change and transform her life (John 4). His words of encouragement and affirmation touched the lives of so many during his earthly ministry.

His words healed and strengthened those who were broken by the weight of their problems. In the synagogue Jesus read the words of the prophet as related in Luke 4:18: "He hath sent me to heal the brokenhearted" (KJV). And when he prayed for people, they began to envision the possibilities God had in store for their lives.

He always built people up and didn't tear people down. At the dinner table with Zacchaeus, the hated tax collector, Jesus showed Zacchaeus the person he could become if only he would open his life to God's grace. He could be changed into the person he was intended to be (Luke 19).

- **Second, What Did He Do?**

He touched people physically, as described in Luke 4:40. There is tremendous power in touch. Medical science has proved that babies will die if they are not touched. Not only did he touch people, but he did more.

He listened to people. He paid attention to their every need. Matthew 15:22-28 describes Jesus with the woman of Canaan. He heard her plea and, acknowledging her faith, healed her daughter.

He forgave those who had lost their way. The woman caught in adultery was given new hope and new direction for her life when he said to her, "Go, and sin no more" (John 8:11 KJV). Jesus truly loved people, and that love changed their lives.

He healed people of all types of diseases and infirmities. The great physician assured them that he would always be with them and he would never desert them. In Matthew 28:20 we read, "Lo, I am with you always, even to the end of the age" (NKJV).

He blessed people, especially little children. Children loved to be around Jesus. They were attracted to him because of his love and his sensitivity to their needs.

On one occasion, after a very busy day, children were thronging to get near Jesus, but the disciples tried to prevent them from approaching him. Jesus saw the situation and said, "Let the little children come to me; do not stop them; for it is to such as these that the kingdom of God belongs" (Mark 10:14).

He gave hope to those with whom he came in contact. When his close friend Lazarus died, he told Lazarus's sisters, Mary and Martha, "I am the resurrection and the life. He who believes in Me, though he may die, he shall live. And whoever lives and believes in Me shall never die" (John 11:25-26 NKJV).

He gave people abundant life as well as the assurance of eternal life. We should think how Jesus Christ would deal specifically with our problem in his earthly ministry. If we find a similar set of circumstances or events in the New Testament, we can trace what he did from the start to the finish as he changed people's lives. We should look for principles, promises, or possibilities contained in the biblical story. We can put ourselves in the passage and imagine what the person must have felt when he or she encountered Jesus Christ. By taking these steps, we can begin to believe it is possible that he can do for us exactly what he did for the person in the biblical narrative. We may sing the words of Stuart Hamblen: "It is no secret what God can do, / What He's done for others, He'll do for you." Indeed, what Christ did for people two thousand years ago he can still do today.

When we are going through a tough time, one of the biggest struggles is to feel God's presence. We think, *Why doesn't he do something? Does he really care about me and those I love?* We must remember that he knows our names. He knows what we are going through. He is there in the midst of it. If God had a refrigerator, our pictures would be on the door. The simple fact that he knows us and what we are going through provides help and comfort and strength. We can tell him about our problem and talk to him as our very best friend. One of the best-loved gospel songs speaks to this issue:

> What a friend we have in Jesus, all our sins and griefs to bear!
> What a privilege to carry everything to God in prayer!
> O what peace we often forfeit, O what needless pain we bear,
> All because we do not carry everything to God in prayer.

He knows what is best for us as we go through a difficult time. His companionship is there for us twenty-four hours a day. What wonderful reassurance and comfort we have in knowing that he is only a prayer away at such a time in our lives.

He cares for us. What a simple but profound statement! If there is any one dominant characteristic of Jesus Christ, it is his compassion, his concern and care for each of us personally. In 1 Peter 5:7 we read, "Cast all your anxiety on him, because he cares for you." Like a good shepherd who cares for his sheep, Jesus Christ gives provision, protection, power, and leadership. His concern is evident in more than mere words; it is expressed in his actions. Hebrews 13:5 repeats the promise of God: "Never will I leave you; never will I forsake you" (NIV). We may have been abandoned by a parent or a spouse, but God will never abandon us. He will never reject us. He will never leave us regardless of the circumstances.

He wants to help us. Many times we do not think we are worthy of being helped. Too many people suffer from extremely low self-esteem. They feel as though they are beyond our Lord's grace. They believe that they are undeserving of being helped. From time to time we mistakenly think, *He may help my friend, but he won't help me.* I've learned that God doesn't play favorites. He reminds us in Matthew 7, "Ask and it will be given to you; seek and you will find; knock and the door will be opened to you" (v. 7 NIV). His help comes in many amazing ways. Sometimes it is through answered prayer; at other times a supernatural intervention reminds us of his concern for us.

Many times in my life he has sent wingless angels—human beings who truly are his angels of mercy. At other times it may be an idea, an invention, or an insight that changes our lives for the good. He may even use a complete stranger as his messenger. At still other times he chooses to use a book, a sermon, a worship service, or a song or other music to speak to our hearts. I will never forget a time in the fall of 1997 when I was going through a very difficult period in my life. I was traveling to a speaking engagement when on the radio I heard for the first time, "God will make a way where there seems to be no way." This song spoke to my heart with such power that I had to pull off to the side of the road and cry as God used this song to minister to me in a very personal and powerful way. How he comes to us is not nearly as important as the simple fact that we can trust and believe that he will come.

Expectantly and Prayerfully Imagine and Anticipate

Expectantly and prayerfully imagine and anticipate the way that he will transform your problem into a possibility. God can transform the problem into a possibility. We believe that he can do it. Through the eyes of faith, we envision how he will do it. In Ephesians 3:20 we read, "Now to him who is able to do immeasurably more than all we ask or imagine, according to his power that is at work within us" (NIV). This powerful passage reminds us that even our wildest imagination cannot begin to compare with how God will work in our lives if we will open ourselves up to his grace. He will do immeasurably more than we can envision.

We must prayerfully imagine his transformational touch and power being released in the midst of our problems. The act of imagining how he will transform a problem is a significant faith builder. We may be guilty of using our imagination negatively to envision a worst-case scenario. Let's reverse the process and believe a best-case scenario. What may at first look impossible will begin to change when we imagine all possible ways that the problem can be solved or the struggle over-come. Faith believes God specializes in turning impossible problems into possibilities. Many times we don't give God a chance to decide whether something is impossible. Whatever the decision, we are not to make it: God must make it.

Negative, fearful, impossibility thinkers are characterized by the following:

- They have to see it before they believe it.
- They can tell us all the reasons that it can't be done or why it is a bad idea, and that someone has tried it and has failed in the past.

- They will always tell us that it will cost too much.
- They are problem imaginers, failure predictors, and worry creators.
- They are optimism deflators and confidence squelchers.

We have to believe it before we see it. If we believe it, we will see it. We will be amazed at what he will bring into our imagination. We will be even more amazed when we persevere in faith and he brings it to pass.

Positive, faith-oriented possibility thinkers have the following characteristics:

- They believe and trust God to turn dreams into exciting adventures.
- They believe and trust that God can turn problems into profitable projects and obstacles into opportunities.
- They experience seeing God turn opportunities into rich enterprises and tragedies into amazing triumphs.

The key issue is whether we will trust him by surrendering our relationships, our problems, our responsibilities, and our struggles into the Lord's hands. The biggest struggle we will face is continuing to try to make it under our own power. We must determine to place our problems into his hands and leave them there, but only after we have done our part. If we do our part, he will do his. Walt Disney was the ultimate problem solver and creative genius. At the dedication of Disney World in Florida, when it was opened to the public, someone said to Mrs. Disney, "I'm so sorry Walt didn't live to see it." She smiled and said, "Oh, but he did!"

When we have done everything that we know to do and placed the problem into God's hands, we acknowledge our total surrender to the Lord Jesus Christ. The results of our trust and our perseverance will be amazing.

* * * * *

Some Thoughts as We Move beyond the Storm

We have made our way from panic and fear to faith and perseverance, but we know that other storms will come as long as we live in this world. Let us remember, then, the obligations we owe to the God whom we have come to know and count on.

- **To praise and thank him in advance**
  It is easy to praise and thank God after the fact, but it takes real faith to thank him before the prayer is

answered, before the dream becomes reality, before the check is deposited in the bank, or before the deal is finalized. Praise and thanksgiving release God's resources, his ideas, and his plans to help us. We never could have imagined, designed, or discovered the solution on our own. His timing is perfect. His answer, his solution, his guidance, and his promise come at just the right moment. When we least expect it, he will break through the impossible obstacle. Isaiah 55:8 speaks to this issue: "My thoughts are not your thoughts, / nor are your ways my ways." We thank him for being the Lord of the impossible. We thank him for transforming our problems into possibilities and our trials into triumphs.

- **To ask God for a specific promise**

We live in a world of broken promises. We make verbal promises, but unfortunately we do not always keep them. Contracts are easily broken, and millions of dollars are spent on legal fees trying to make people live up to their promises or their commitments. When we are trying to solve a tough, giant-sized problem, it is essential to have a promise from God. When God makes a promise to us, we can trust him completely to fulfill his commitment. God's promise is found in the Scripture and confirmed by the Holy Spirit in our minds and hearts. Isaiah 43:2 cites one of God's most comforting promises in the entire Bible: "I will be with you." Talk about giving us confidence and courage as we go through our struggles! Regardless of what we may be going through, he promises to be there, protecting us and providing for us.

Every problem has a promise from God, who is the ultimate promise keeper. The greater the problem or struggle, the greater the promise from God's word. God's promises are reserved for his children. God's promises are activated by our faith and carried out in obedience. We are given a choice: Will we believe and trust in God's promises, or will we question and doubt what he has said? James 1:6-7 states, "Let him ask in faith, with no doubting, for he who doubts is like a wave of the sea driven and tossed by the wind. For let not that man suppose that he will receive anything from the Lord" (NKJV). God's children acclaim and obey his promises.

- **To look beyond the problem**

This visualization of the future without the problem is really hard to accomplish, especially if we are in the middle of a major battle and want to give up and quit. This step is an excellent way to help us endure what we have to go through. The good news is, there is life on the other side—let's visualize it.

One of the most discouraging and defeating thoughts is, *This is the way my life is always going to be. I am forever sentenced to a life trapped in the pain and helplessness and hopelessness of my current problem.* Nothing could be farther from the truth. This is the promise of the Lord. There is a better life on the other side of the storm that we are facing. We must continue to pursue and persevere. When an older gentleman was asked, "What is your favorite passage of Scripture?" he smiled and replied, "And it came to pass." All problems have a limited lifetime. They, too, will pass. Remember: the battle is not ours but the Lord's! We will make it **through the storm!**

Worth Remembering

- "Nothing in the world can take the place of persistence. Talent will not; nothing is more common than unsuccessful men with talent. Genius will not; unrewarded genius is almost a proverb. Education will not; the world is full of educated derelicts. **Persistence and determination alone are omnipotent**" (Calvin Coolidge).
- Learn from the past, live in the present, and look forward to the future.
- "Every adversity, every failure, and any heartbreak carry with them the seeds of an equivalent or greater benefit" (Napoleon Hill).

- Expectantly and prayerfully imagine and anticipate the way God will transform your problem into a possibility.
- "My thoughts are not your thoughts, / nor are your ways my ways" (Isaiah 55:8).
- Remember: the battle is not ours but the Lord's.

Questions

1. How has God whispered in your storm?
2. When have you been tempted to quit or give up?
3. How were you able to persevere?
4. What made it difficult for you to trust and rely unconditionally on God?
5. Imagine how Jesus Christ might have dealt with your problem in his earthly ministry. What would that look like today?
6. How can you praise and thank God as you move beyond the storm?
7. On which of God's promises have you depended in order to get through your storm?

Power Connection

Lord, help me hear your whispers as I go through my storm. Tune my heart to hear you as you speak. Give me grace to follow and depend totally on you. Thank you that there is a better life on the other side of the storm. May I never give up or quit. Amen.